Why Be Catholic?

Why Be Catholic?

UNDERSTANDING OUR
EXPERIENCE AND TRADITION

Richard Rohr
and
Joseph Martos

Nihil Obstat: Rev. Lawrence Landini, O.F.M.
Rev. Edward Gratsch

Imprimi Potest: Rev. Jeremy Harrington, O.F.M.
Provincial

Imprimatur: +James H. Garland, V.G.
Archdiocese of Cincinnati
June 15, 1989

The *nihil obstat* and *imprimatur* are a declaration that a book is considered to be free from doctrinal or moral error. It is not implied that those who have granted the *nihil obstat* and *imprimatur* agree with the contents, opinions or statements expressed.

The excerpt from *Children of Sanchez: Autobiography of A Mexican Family,* ©1961 by Oscar Lewis, is reprinted by permission of Random House, Inc.

The excerpt from *Catholicism,* by Richard P. McBrien, ©1981 by Richard McBrien, is reprinted by permission of Harper & Row, Publishers, Inc.

Scripture citations are the authors' paraphrase.

Cover and book design by Julie Lonneman

ISBN 0-86716-101-9

Preface

In 1985 Franciscan Father Richard Rohr presented four talks at St. Francis Renewal Center in Cincinnati, Ohio. He spoke on a topic of increasing concern to many people during the closing decades of the 20th century: the meaning of their identification with the Christian tradition and the purpose of their membership in the Roman Catholic Church.

Following the Second Vatican Council in the 1960's, Catholics began to wonder about their uniqueness within the broader Christian tradition and to question the value of working within the institutional structures of Catholicism. Conservative Catholics asked whether the Church was giving up too much too fast, and liberal Catholics asked why the Church was not changing faster.

In the 1970's the spirit of ecumenism softened the sharp divisions between Protestantism and Catholicism. Ecumenical dialogue with the "separated brethren" reduced the tension that had existed between the churches since the Protestant Reformation, and it overcame the bitterness of four centuries of religious rivalry. But ecumenism also led well-meaning Christians on both sides of the dialogue to ask whether the Catholic Church was really as unique as it once appeared. Could it be that Catholicism was just one valid way to be Christian, without any real claim to superiority or privilege?

The spirit of reform in the first years after the Council eliminated much that had been uniquely Catholic in the Church's public life: the unchanging Latin Mass and sacraments, statues of saints and devotions to the Blessed Mother, clerical clothing and religious dress, rigid adherence to Church laws and unswerving obedience to the pope, to name a few. During the 1980's the pace of practical reform slowed down, however, and those who viewed many traditional Catholic practices as antiquated saw their hopes of Church renewal fading. Could it be, they asked, that

Catholicism is institutionally incapable of honest and thorough ongoing reform?

On both the right and the left, therefore, Catholics have been wondering about the Church and their role in it. Richard Rohr, as pastor of New Jerusalem Community in Cincinnati, felt that tension both within his community and within the Archdiocese of Cincinnati. I, as theologian and teacher at Xavier University, experienced it both within the academic world and within the pastoral world of parish life. No place or group is immune from the soul-searching going on within the Church about the Church.

At the extremes of both right and left, some people have felt so strongly that the Catholic Church is not what it ought to be that they have severed their ties with it. Some have chosen to start churches of their own, claiming they are thus preserving "true" Catholicism. Some have chosen to join other churches, claiming Roman Catholicism has lost touch with "true" Christianity.

Richard Rohr and I believe that the truth is to be found in that broad middle ground where tension is experienced the most. The truth is to be lived not by giving in to the temptation to escape to the extremes but by accepting the Catholic heritage while working to change the institutional Church from within. By being truthful to the broad tradition of the past, we can hope to influence its course in the future.

Those who listened to Richard's talks in 1985 came to understand how challenging it is to be truly Catholic. When I listened to the tapes of those talks, I felt that Richard's understanding deserved to reach a wider audience. With his permission and the encouragement of St. Anthony Messenger Press, I took on the task of editing those tapes and writing a book that expresses the understanding we both have about the tradition we call our own.

I hope that those who read this book will appreciate more fully the challenge of being deeply rooted in the past while moving with the Catholic Church into the 21st century.

Joseph Martos
Allentown College

Contents

Introduction

Why be Catholic?

That is a question Catholics never asked a generation ago. People who were thinking about joining the Catholic Church may have asked it, but not Catholics themselves. If you were born Catholic, you simply accepted the faith, its traditions and beliefs.

The Church gave those of us who were born and raised Catholics a strong sense of identity. Catholicism told us who and what we were as human beings, as Christians, even as individuals. We were nurtured and sustained by that great maternal institution known respectfully as Holy Mother Church.

Catholicism was a total worldview, a total system of thinking, feeling and behaving. You could just as easily stop being Catholic as you could stop being black—which is to say you really could not. You might formally leave the institution, but you could not change the way you had been taught to look at the world, God, religion or yourself.

Today the Catholic Church is much different from a generation ago. Pope John XXIII's program of *aggiornamento* or "updating" succeeded far better than anyone imagined. American Catholicism, in particular, is very different from what it was prior to the 1960's. The Second Vatican Council ushered in an era of ecumenism which broke down many barriers between the Catholic Church and other Christian denominations.

The greater openness of the Church is good, and the greater acceptance of others is good. But a Church without walls also has a harder time defining itself. Today it is not so easy to say what makes Roman Catholicism different from other forms of Christianity.

Young Catholics today—those who have grown up considering the changes of Vatican II "normal"—do not have nearly the sense of religious identity that their parents did.

They do not see much real difference between their church and the churches that their friends belong to. At some point in their life, usually in early adulthood, they have to face seriously the question, Why be Catholic?

Older Catholics today, too, sometimes find themselves wondering about the Church. For any number of reasons, they can feel themselves being tempted to leave and join some other church. In their case the question is more like, Why remain Catholic?

No matter which way the question is put, it requires an answer.

The answer to that question, however, cannot be simple. The Catholic Church is not a small institution. The Catholic faith is not an easily recited set of beliefs. The Catholic heritage is not a brief tradition.

To answer the question fairly and squarely, we have to treat the good and the bad. We have to develop an appreciation about what is good in Catholicism, but we also have to be honest about the Church's shortcomings. Chapters One and Two address these two issues.

To answer the question for American Catholics, we have to look at what it means to be Catholic in the United States today. We have to come to a sense of how we can live with a mature faith in our society as it moves into the 21st century. Chapter Three deals with being Catholic in the United States.

Finally, to answer the question in a more personal way, we have to ask what kind of person we can expect to become if we take our Catholic faith seriously. We have to look carefully at the lives of those people who have found personal fulfillment by living their faith to the utmost. Chapter Four presents pictures of outstanding Catholics, especially those we call saints.

Even by getting at the answer to our question in four different ways, we will not have exhausted the topic. Being Catholic means more than what can be said in four short chapters. At least, however, we will have made a start at answering that question. From there we each need to add our own reasons for being, or remaining, Catholic.

Chapter One

What's Great About Being Catholic?

Tradition.

The answer to this chapter's question can be given in that single word: *tradition*. When most people hear that word today, however, they miss so much of what it implies. They tend to think not of tradition but of *traditions*.

Traditions, by and large, are the ways we do things from one year to the next. Individuals and families, parishes and schools, cities and countries, even companies and other institutions, have their own traditions. A family might have a tradition of gathering with all the relatives at Thanksgiving. A company might have a tradition of celebrating its founding with an outdoor fair and picnic.

Traditions are particular and they can change. The Catholic Church, for example, once used Greek, then Latin, in its public worship. The more recent tradition is to pray in one's native language.

In the deeper sense of the word, a tradition is much more pervasive and long-lasting than those traditions just mentioned. The word itself comes from the Latin *tradere*, which means to hand over. Even short traditions get handed over from one year to the next. A long tradition is passed from one century to the next, shaping and enriching each new generation.

A culture is a tradition in this deeper sense of the word. We can think of cultures geographically, like European or Middle Eastern or Southeast Asian. We also can think of cultures ethnically, like Spanish or German or Japanese. Finally, we can focus on some aspect of life and speak of religion or politics or technology as traditional.

Catholicism is a tradition in that deeper cultural sense. It is a whole way of thinking and feeling about life and God and oneself, and a way of behaving and responding to people and situations. Even so, Catholicism is but part of a much broader and longer tradition—the Judeo-Christian tradition, which has been greatly influenced by Western European culture.

Catholicism is thus a religious tradition with both Eastern and Western cultural elements. Although Judaism and early Christianity began in the Middle East, the Church has been predominantly Western since the conversion of the Roman Empire in the fourth century and the evangelization of Europe beginning in the seventh century.

Our tradition is rather like a great tree with Eastern roots transplanted into Western soil and fertilized by European nutrients. As an Eastern tradition, Christianity is a wisdom tradition. It is a way of life, a way of relating to God and others in a manner which embodies the wisdom of the ancient world. It is a spiritual tradition of personal growth and interpersonal relationships whose greatest expression is the Bible. Both the Old and New Testaments are primarily concerned with how people should live in relationship with God and one another in order to find true fulfillment and ultimate happiness.

As a Western tradition, Christianity is a practical tradition. The genius of the Roman Empire was its pragmatic ability to govern many diverse groups and keep them at peace with one another. Catholicism inherited this gift of organization and used it to evangelize Europe and to administer the Church in the Middle Ages. It found a way to preserve the wisdom of the Scriptures while establishing the faith in the Western world.

Every gardener knows that the right amount of fertilizer can enhance a tree's growth and increase its fruitfulness and that too much fertilizer can damage roots and decrease fruitfulness. Unfortunately, the impact of Western culture on

Christianity has damaged our religious roots.

Both Catholicism and Protestantism (which grew out of Catholicism in the 16th century) have suffered from this damage to our Eastern roots. Our forgetfulness of our Jewish heritage caused the antagonism of Christians towards Jews. Our disregard for the wisdom of the Scriptures, especially the lessons of the prophets and the Gospels, caused the European permissiveness towards war. Our neglect of the teachings of Jesus and the example of the earliest Christians caused the Western tolerance of the pursuit of wealth.

In our tradition, the pragmatism of the West often overshadows the spirituality of the East. The Western mind is oriented outward, toward the world around. It loves to discover and analyze and create new things. Modern science and technology are products of Western thinking. The Eastern mind, on the other hand, is oriented inward, toward the human heart and soul. It prefers to focus on the inner world of the spirit, the center of feelings and values and attitudes. Western Christianity, both Protestant and Catholic, has been predominantly functional and institutional rather than spiritual and personal.

Catholicism at its best has combined the spirituality of the East and the practicality of the West in growing and fruitful ways. It has produced spiritual giants in its saints, intellectual giants in its great theologians and administrative giants in many of its bishops and popes. It has given rise to great movements such as monasticism, scholasticism and religious orders at those very times when the world needed them the most. It has been a dynamic tradition of practical spirituality, of wisdom put into practice.

Catholicism at its worst has not maintained the synthesis between Eastern and Western thinking. When the balance has become upset, most often it has tilted in the direction of Western pragmatism. Then it has been narrow and legalistic, authoritarian and controlling, impersonal and utilitarian. It has sometimes been a rigid tradition of institutional functionalism.

We cannot understand the entire Catholic tradition without looking carefully at both its successes and its failures, its greatness and its weakness. In Chapter Two we shall look honestly at the dark side of Catholicism. Now, however, let us examine more closely the bright side of our tradition.

The Appreciation of Creation

Catholicism traditionally has been open to the goodness of the world and all of God's creation. A poem by Hilaire Belloc claims:

> Wherever a Catholic sun doth shine,
> There's plenty of laughter and good red wine.
> At least, I've always found it so:
> *Benedicamus Domino!*

The last line, Latin for "Let us bless the Lord!," expresses gratefulness for the good things of life and thankfulness to the author of creation. In its own way this poem repeats what the Bible says about the sixth day of the creation of the world:

> God looked at everything he had made, and he found it very good (Genesis 1:31).

At bottom, the Catholic tradition is in touch with the goodness of the world and the joyfulness of life. It tells us to rejoice and be glad for all the great and small pleasures that come to us from God through creation. It has little in common with the Puritan belief that pleasure is sinful and that beauty is a temptation from the devil.

If we are honest, though, we have to admit that Puritanism has sometimes infected the Catholic outlook. Sixteenth-century Protestants charged the Catholic Church with corruption and worldliness, and in reaction Catholics tried to outdo the Puritans in purity, especially in sexual morality. Sometimes we have been more puritanical than Catholic in our attitude towards sex and other physical pleasures.

From time to time some Christians have not believed in a full goodness of creation. Early Gnostics and other "super spiritual" groups felt that the material world was evil, but they were regarded as heretics by the majority of Christians. In the Middle Ages some monks thought that sex was sinful, but the Church replied by affirming the sacramentality of marriage. A few centuries later Catholic Puritans (called Jansenists) condemned all worldliness and sensuality, but the Church officially rejected their teaching.

Those of us who come from northern European backgrounds (especially Irish and German) inherited this Jansenistic negativity anyway. Priests and nuns often portrayed sexual misconduct as the worst possible sin. As Americans we also adopted a good deal of Puritanism from our Protestant neighbors. Our immigrant grandparents didn't want to appear to be less moral than the people around them!

The older Catholic tradition, however, has Mediterranean roots. Palestinians and Greeks, Italians and French, Spaniards and Portuguese have always been more comfortable with their bodies than northern Europeans. Peasants and poor people in most "Catholic countries" have always appreciated the good things that nature has to offer. Food and drink, sex and children are the simple but most basic pleasures that life can give us. They are, after all, gifts from God.

This is why Catholicism is fundamentally sacramental. A sacrament is a sign of God's goodness to us. Catholic wisdom says that the world and everything in it is a gift from God and a sign of God. The seven sacraments we celebrate in church use water and oil, bread and wine, and human touch as signs of God's graciousness. Catholics see God shining through all of creation, and so the Church uses the gifts of creation in its most important rituals.

Another way to say this is that for Catholicism and for the longer Judeo-Christian tradition, flesh mediates spirit. The body is the medium through which the human person develops psychologically and intellectually and spiritually. The material world is a channel of God's grace, for through the good things of this world we experience the goodness of God. We can even say that creation is the cosmic medium of God's artistic Spirit. It is the canvas on which God paints so that we can perceive with our hearts the divine beauty that we cannot see with our eyes.

Still another way to say this is that Catholic theology is incarnational. When we hear of incarnation we immediately think of Jesus, God's word made flesh. We take the incarnation much more seriously than those who think that Jesus was God on the inside and human on the outside—a sort of supernatural Clark Kent who looked human but who underneath was an almighty being. The Catholic interpretation of the incarnation since the earliest councils of the Church has been that Jesus was both fully human and fully divine—not 50 percent God and 50 percent man but 100 percent human as well as 100 percent divine.

If Jesus is the incarnation of God, Jesus is also the revelation of God. In Jesus the mystery of God is revealed in a way that we can see it, even if we don't completely comprehend it. In the life of Jesus God's life of grace is manifested. In the words of Jesus God communicates to us in ways that we can hear. In the deeds of Jesus God's activity in the world is demonstrated. In the love of Jesus God shows us what divine love is really like. In the death and resurrection of Jesus God reveals the secret of our ultimate redemption.

Because Jesus is the ultimate revelation of God, Jesus is the fundamental sacrament of God. He is the greatest sign of God's love and presence and activity in the world. The sacramentality of Jesus did not end with the ascension, however. It continues in the Church which, since the days of St. Paul, has been called the Body of Christ. The Church as the whole People of God under the headship of Christ incarnates the divine presence in creation, similar to the way that Jesus did this as a single individual. The Church is basically a sacrament of God in the world.

This is why the Catholic Church emphasizes the sacraments so much. We believe that, just as people 2,000 years ago came in contact with God when they allowed themselves to be touched by Jesus, people today come in contact with God when they are touched by water and oil and human hands. We put something as simple and basic as a meal of bread and wine at the center of our worship. The Eucharist is the Catholic way of saying that the way to God is not primarily through private meditation but through sharing food with one another. Our worship is not so much verbal and intellectual but physical and relational. The liturgy is a communal celebration of a down-to-earth reality—our sharing the life of Christ with one another.

In contrast, Protestant churches have tended to emphasize the Bible. They took the altar table out of the center of Christian worship and put the pulpit in its place. Preaching the Scriptures is important, but it results in a style of worship that is more verbal than sacramental.

Also by way of contrast, Eastern religions such as Hinduism and Buddhism tend to emphasize meditation. They take the community dimension out of worship and make it individual. Personal prayer is important, but meditation by itself leads to a style of religion that is more private than communal, more intellectual than incarnational.

The Catholic tradition, which is reflected both in its theology and in its worship, is incarnational and sacramental. It takes the world seriously and encourages us to find God in the world. It takes human activity seriously and encourages us to be like Jesus in the world. The Church has consistently taught social justice because it believes that God's righteousness should be not just talked about but incarnated in the world of human affairs.

We can also see the Catholic appreciation for creation in the world of Christian art. Religious mosaics and sculptures date from Roman times. Medieval Christians expressed their faith in towering Gothic cathedrals and colorful stained glass windows. The Renaissance (which began in Italy) gave religious art and architecture (such as St. Peter's in Rome) a new dimension of magnificence. Nor should we forget that modern music developed out of Gregorian chant and that modern drama began with medieval religious plays. Catholic wisdom appreciates the goodness not just in God's creation but also in human creativity.

A Universal Vision

The original meaning of the word *catholic* is "universal." The Church was first called catholic in ancient times when Christianity had spread throughout the Roman Empire. The first universal Church council met in the year 325, and in similar councils the world's bishops formulated the Church's catholic faith. The summary of that worldwide faith is the Nicene Creed—named after the Council of Nicea—which we say at Mass every Sunday.

The Catholic Church still has a worldwide faith, and the Church's vision is still universal. We glimpse this in the world travels of Pope John Paul II. We see him greeting and being welcomed by North, Central and South Americans, by Europeans, Asians and Africans. We hear him speaking many languages, but his message is always the universal faith of the Church. The Pope's vision looks beyond national boundaries and sees the unity of all people in Christ.

The Catholic Church is not a national church. Like the United Nations, it is one of the few truly international institutions in the world today. Like the Red Cross, it puts the needs of people ahead of national identity or political ideology. Especially in Third World countries, the Church is in a unique position to mediate between the political left and right. Because it does not belong to any one country, the Church can bring a broader vision to disputes between rival factions aligned with the United States or the Soviet Union.

The Catholic Church is also a multicultural church. In the past Catholicism flourished in the ancient culture of the Middle East, the Mediterranean culture of the Roman Empire, the medieval culture of Western Europe and the modern culture of Europe and America. Today Catholicism is not just European and American but also Latin and African and Asian. Wherever you travel you can meet Catholic brothers and sisters celebrating their faith in Christ in their own unique cultural styles. People of every race and culture embrace the Catholic faith and are embraced by the universal Church.

Because the Church is universal, it calls us to a universal vision. As the world gets smaller every year, we need to regard everyone in it as our neighbor. We are beginning to realize that culturally, politically and economically we cannot pretend that the world revolves around the United States. The Church has long realized that governments need to look beyond their own self-interest to meet the needs of God's people everywhere. Our faith is already larger than most of us appreciate, challenging our narrowness and preparing us for global responsibility.

The pastoral letters of the U.S. Catholic Bishops, *The Challenge of Peace* and *Economic Justice for All*, reflect this global outlook, as does Pope John Paul II's encyclical *On Social Concerns*. The bishops and the Pope remind us that the peace of Christ cannot be enforced by military might and that the justice of God's Kingdom cannot be produced by either communism or capitalism. The peace of Christ means harmony, not tension, and the justice of God means cooperation, not competition.

Too many Catholics today do not have this universal vision, and so their faith is not truly catholic. They have a narrow, provincial outlook instead of a genuinely Catholic worldview. They do not understand that to be Catholic means to be Christian first and American second. They do not put the invitation of the gospel ahead of the demands of nationalism. They fall into the idolatry condemned by the prophets and rejected by Jesus.

By failing to be truly catholic in their vision, these Catholics betray their own tradition. They make Catholicism appear to be no different from any other nationalistic church. More than this, they get bound up by their own self-interest and surrender the freedom that comes from being able to make disinterested, honest judgments.

Catholics ought to be free to judge politics and economics from a broader perspective that cuts across historical and national boundaries. The Catholic tradition transcends petty politics and shortsighted policies.

If we are truly Catholic, we must look at the world and all people in it from God's perspective, not from a self-centered point of view. The Catholic vision is the same as God's concern for the entire human family.

A Holistic Outlook

Catholicism's breadth of vision naturally leads to a holistic outlook on reality. Catholic thinkers look at life from many different perspectives and try to see the unity that ties all of them together. No human being can look at the universe from every possible angle all at once. Only God's knowledge embraces all of reality in a single cosmic vision. In the Catholic tradition, however, philosophers and theologians look at things from various perspectives in order to develop a sense of the whole.

This Catholic sense about the interconnectedness of all reality is the basis of what we call theology, or the attempt to see the connections between our Christian faith and what we can find out from scientific research and our own experience. After philosophy (which dates back to pre-Christian times), the oldest intellectual discipline in the world is theology. One of the earliest definitions of theology is "faith seeking understanding." The Catholic ideal is to trust in God, believe what the Scriptures reveal and accept what the Church teaches, while respecting reason and logic, and promoting inquiry and understanding.

When barbarian tribes swept across Europe and caused the fall of the Roman Empire, monks carefully copied fragile manuscripts so that ancient science would not be lost. In the Middle Ages Christian scholars founded schools which eventually became the great universities of Europe. Despite the obtuseness of the Church officials who condemned Galileo for proposing that the sun did not revolve around the earth, modern science grew out of the efforts of Christians to understand the universe that God created.

St. Augustine tried to understand all of history from the perspective of Catholic faith. St. Thomas Aquinas studied all medieval science before writing his great *Summa Theologica*, a four-volume "summary" of theology. Other Catholic scholars advanced medicine, law, astronomy and biology. Catholics believe that if they are firmly grounded in their faith, they do not have to feel threatened by any scientific knowledge. Teilhard de Chardin integrated evolution into his Christian understanding of the cosmos.

This cosmic Catholic vision sometimes approaches a mystical intuition about how the whole of creation is ordered by the divine arrangement of God. St. Thomas had a mystical experience toward the end of his theological career, and many of Teilhard's writings have a mystical air about them. The saints whom the Church recognizes as having been great mystics, such as Teresa of Avila and John of the Cross, experienced how the whole of human life takes place within God's plan for the universe. In their own way they were into ecology, seeing the connections between the natural and supernatural orders, even before the word *ecology* became fashionable.

If the Catholic tradition had remained purely Eastern, it would perhaps have stayed purely mystical. The Eastern Christianity of the Orthodox churches has a very mystical flavor to it. Having been influenced by Western culture, however, the Catholic intellectual tradition is also scientific and practical. It likes to ask questions, propose theories, do research and put ideas into practice. Catholic theologians make use of linguistics and archaeology to understand the Bible; they delve into history and anthropology to understand human nature; they utilize psychology and sociology to understand people's behavior; and they accept ideas from economics and politics to understand the modern world in which the Church finds itself. Catholic scientists believe that there are no ultimate contradictions between the discoveries of physics, chemistry and biology on the one hand and God's revelation on the other hand. Catholic educators integrate secular educational theory into their teaching of religion. And Catholic administrators are not afraid to borrow modern management techniques to help them in running the Church's institutions. The Catholic approach to life on all levels is holistic and integrative.

This openness to the totality of human knowledge is not true of all Christians today. Some fundamentalists close their eyes against the evidence for evolution, claiming that it goes against the account of creation given in the Book of Genesis. Other Protestants insist so strongly on the truth of the Bible that they have little respect for what the human sciences can teach us. Some charismatics put so much emphasis on personal religious experience (such as the experience of being "born again") that they do not think about Christian social responsibility. And there are those in all denominations who are legalistic and rigid in their approach to morality.

Catholics, of course, are not immune to these types of shortsightedness. If they forget or have never acquired the holistic outlook of the Catholic tradition, they can be just as fundamentalistic, closed-minded and legalistic as other Christians.

Catholics who understand and appreciate the breadth of their tradition, however, have an admirable ability to pull everything together and see its underlying unity. For the broader Catholic wisdom is that all truth comes from God, whether it is revealed or discovered.

An Invitation of Personal Holiness

The holistic outlook just discussed is not only intellectual and theoretical but also personally practical. The wisdom of the Catholic tradition is that the whole of one's personal life ought to be as richly rewarding as God intended. God made us to be happy—to live in the Kingdom (to use the biblical phrase) and to live up to our fullest spiritual potential (to use modern terms).

The Church has always been concerned with holiness. At times people have equated holiness with becoming a plaster saint, aloof from others and abstracted from life. Today we realize that holiness is wholeness, that true sanctity is fulfilling the sacred trust that God has given us to become all that God wants us to be. When we are born, our life is pure potential. Actualizing that potential is our basic task in life. Fulfilling that potential, especially the spiritual dimensions of it, is to become truly whole, or holy. The words "whole" and "holy" come from the same root.

The Catholic wisdom tradition has never said that you

need to be a secluded monk or a cloistered nun to be holy. In the past Catholicism presented monks and nuns and priests as ideals, due in no small part to the fact that society in the Middle Ages considered these the educated people. They had the opportunity to read and learn, to meditate on the Scriptures and to pray—at a time when people had to eke out an existence without benefits of modern science and industry.

Nevertheless, if we look at the Church's calendar of saints, we see fishermen and farmers, husbands and wives, rich and poor, soldiers and scholars, even kings and queens honored there. Everyone is called to achieve his or her fullest potential, to be a truly whole and holy person, regardless of occupation or state of life.

Some of the greatest examples of this holistic achievement are the mystics. St. Teresa of Avila was the most liberated woman of her day. She traveled around Spain in the 16th century renewing monastic life, energized by daily meditation and communication with God in prayer. St. Francis of Assisi possessed an inner freedom and an outer simplicity so attractive to others that before he died thousands of men and women had adopted the Franciscan life-style. Saints and mystics have a holistic outlook on life that is refreshing. They see themselves for what they are and invite God to make them all they can be.

This holistic spirituality is rewarding but also demanding. Catholic holiness is not a Jesus-and-me attitude. It is not enough to go to church on Sunday and leave the rest of your life unchanged. True holiness requires a conversion of the whole person, a transformation of the total personality. And it requires a conversion of your life-style, no matter where you live or what you do for a living.

Everyone today wants to be happy. People search for it in wealth, power and success, and when these fail to make them truly happy they look for happiness in other ways. Some have even discovered the benefits of meditation, but sometimes secular meditation leads to withdrawing from life rather than fully entering into it. The wisdom of the Catholic tradition is that activity in the world and communication with

God are both needed to give meaning and energy to the whole of life.

The Catholic understanding of human development begins with conversion, but it also affirms that conversion has to be ongoing. Christian life is a process of continuous conversion and growth into a more and more Christ-like personality. There is no one moment when a Catholic claims to be "saved," as some evangelical Protestants do. The stories of the saints show that they continuously strove for holiness. Even the Catholic devotion known as the Stations of the Cross suggests that Christian life is a process, a journey that goes through stages, introducing us to different challenges, pitfalls and personalities along the way. Those who persevere in fidelity and trust enter more deeply into the life of Christ.

Fortunately, our salvation and our happiness do not depend on us alone. God is with us and lovingly takes the initiative in offering us salvation and calling us to holiness. This is the meaning of grace. Grace is God's invitation and power reaching into us. But we have to open ourselves to God in order to be filled with the Spirit. We have to cooperate with the grace that is offered in order to live grace-filled lives.

Curiously, our cooperation is not so much a "doing" as a "not doing." The wisdom of the saints is that they stopped long enough to listen to God in their hearts and let God tell them how to be truly happy. Growth in the Spirit, growth in spiritual perfection (as we used to call it), is the same as growing in Christ. It means surrendering our limited image of what we can be and entering into the process of becoming like Christ, while also becoming our true self.

Paradoxically, personal fulfillment means abandoning ourselves and putting others first. It means moving beyond wanting to be loved and moving into becoming lovers. It means growing past our need for things and discovering happiness in giving things away—even giving ourselves away, as Jesus did.

In the Catholic tradition ultimate satisfaction is promised to those who give up their false and private self for the true and whole self that is found in God. Jesus promises that

"Those who seek their own life will lose it, but those who give up their life will find it" (Mark 8:35). This is part of the meaning of crucifixion, for the cross leads to resurrection, to new life.

When we let go of ourselves, we let ourselves be caught by God. When we stop directing our lives, we let ourselves be taught by God. When we stop trying to fix and fulfill ourselves, we can allow our lives to be filled by grace. The lives of St. Francis of Assisi, Pope John XXIII and Mother Teresa of Calcutta radiate a grace that even non-Catholics admire. Catholic wisdom is that the life of free will and grace is the greatest fulfillment that a person can experience.

An Experience of Community

It is difficult to hear the Lord calling us to holiness in isolation and almost impossible to respond to that vocation if we try to go it alone. St. Paul noted that "Faith comes through hearing, and hearing comes through those who bring us the good news of salvation" (Romans 10:17). He was not referring just to hearing with our ears but also to that deeper listening we have to do in our hearts. It is hard to get a sense of God's promise of fulfillment unless we experience that promise being fulfilled in the lives of people around us. It is even harder to do the "not doing" of personal surrender to the Lord without the guidance of others who have done it and without the support of others who will meet the needs we have given up trying to meet for ourselves.

Our immigrant grandparents had a wonderful sense of Catholic togetherness in the ethnic parishes of large cities and in the rural parishes of farming and mining towns. Catholics grew up with one another, went to school together, worked together and worshiped together. Parishes were small enough that the pastor knew everyone by name and neighborly enough that people provided for one another's needs. They were still living the tradition of community brought with them from Catholic Europe.

The great medieval cathedrals of Europe were built not

by construction companies but by Christians who wanted to express their faith in a work of their own hands. Some of those cathedrals took a hundred years or more to complete. Generations of stonecutters, carpenters and glassmakers dedicated their time and talents to the communal effort, while other townspeople supplied food and materials for the workers.

The same was true in early America. The Cathedral of the Plains in western Kansas, where Richard Rohr's parents were married, was built by Catholic families who settled that territory. Every month fathers and sons hauled wagonloads of stone to the site, and every year they could see the fruit of their efforts taking shape. When the church was completed, those German Catholics in Kansas had a real sense that this place of worship expressed who they were as a community.

To a great extent, we in America have lost that Catholic sense of community. We have become part of the mobile society that does not stay long enough in one place to put down roots. The people we see most often every day probably do not attend the same church we do. Many parishes are so huge that they are run like a business, impersonally. At Sunday Mass many people feel more like an anonymous audience than like a faith community.

Most American Catholics live their faith lives alone. If they know about struggles others are having with their faith, most likely it is through reading about it in books and magazines, not from other people themselves. Most Catholics do not share their questions and insights nor their difficulties and triumphs with others who have had the same thoughts and experiences. Catholics, for the most part, do not pray together or study the Scriptures together. They do not relax together or just spend time getting to know one another better.

One reason for this is that as Americans we have bought into the myths of rugged individualism and middle-class success. We believe that we have to make it on our own, and that if we are successful we should have our own separate house, our own private cars and all the appliances to live comfortably by ourselves. To be successful in our society

18

means to be independent, and we are suspicious of people who have to depend on others for support.

This myth of individualistic success is disastrous for community. People pay the price of self-sufficiency by having to make do without relationships that would enrich their lives. Poor people have to do without adequate housing, work, education, transportation and even food. Rich people have to do without the joy that comes with living close to others and sharing the necessities of life. Old people have to do without friends and family who cannot or will not come to visit. Children have to do without parents who must work to try to make ends meet. Most people feel alone in life, and so they turn to alcohol, drugs, television, sex, food, gambling and luxuries to relieve their sense of aloneness.

A truly Christian way of living, by contrast, is communitarian. Early Christians were so connected to one another that St. Paul called each community a "body of Christ." Each local group of Christians was a social body whose soul was the spirit of Christ. Living like Christ meant putting yourself out for one another, making sacrifices for one another, laying down your life for one another. Just as an arm or leg, a mouth or stomach cannot live on its own, Christians did not try to make it on their own. Each one contributed to the common good, and each received the particular things needed to live happily, whether food or clothing, spiritual direction or emotional support.

Even the ancient Greeks who lived before the time of Christ were aware that community was needed for truly human living. Their word for a person who had no idea of the common good was *idios*. In their eyes an individual who lived just for himself without caring for the well-being of others was a moral idiot. In our society, on the contrary, an individual who accumulates great wealth without caring about what happens to others is regarded as a financial genius.

Christianity built on that ancient sense of community and went beyond it. Jesus taught that by not worrying about the things of this world but by caring for other people instead, all our bodily and spiritual needs would be met. To the people in ancient times (who were just as tempted as people today to look out for their own self-interest), this was "the good news of God's Kingdom." Wherever people care for one another the way the Father cares for everyone, they are living in God's Kingdom. That's good news to anyone, then or now, who has ever felt the need to make it on one's own.

When the Church grew so large that this sense of community was in danger of being lost, some Christians who wanted to hold on to this awareness of God's Kingdom left the cities and lived together in the countryside. They worked and prayed and supported one another in what then were called monasteries and what today we might call Christian communes. They were places where Christians supported one another in a communal life-style.

Monasteries became centers of Christian living all around Europe in the Middle Ages. They preserved the wisdom of the ancient world after the fall of the Roman Empire and laid the foundation for the revival of civilization. Many medieval cathedrals were built next to monasteries that inspired people to work together for the common good and the glory of God.

Many European cities also owe their location and original design to the Catholic sense of community. The traditional European city, with its cathedral at the center, the large plaza in front, the promenades all around and the fountains where people could draw water for themselves and their livestock—the very architecture of such cities spoke of unity of life around a common focus of attention. People met and discussed the day's affairs and worked and conducted their business, all within walking distance of where they lived.

In the course of time community-minded Christians discovered other ways of joining their lives together, even in the largest cities. Whenever Western civilization grew to the point that it was becoming impersonal again, the Spirit of Jesus led people to form communities. Usually these communities focused on some special apostolic work, such as caring for the sick, the homeless, or the uneducated. These communities called themselves "religious orders" rather than monasteries because they ordered their lives according to a religious rule even though they did not all live in the same place.

Today, when many of our traditional orders have grown to institutional proportions, Catholics are searching for new forms of communal life. Many in religious orders are moving into smaller, more personal living arrangements. Prayer groups, spiritual movements and base communities are all attempts to revive this Catholic charism in a modern setting.

In our individualistic society there is a great need for this gift of community. Living together in the spirit of Jesus and in the manner of the early Church is the particularly Catholic gift to Western culture. Protestantism by and large lost that gift because of its insistence on individual accountability for one's life before God. The Protestant work ethic, since the founding of this country, has been that one's spiritual salvation is reflected in one's material well-being. This led to a great emphasis on personal success through economic competition, often without regard for the welfare of others.

Our American society has been shaped more by the Protestant than by the Catholic tradition, and Catholics in their desire to be American have unconsciously adopted this Protestant outlook. The Catholic liturgy speaks of community and many sermons address the subject of community, but most Catholics listen with very individualistic ears. Even when moved to step in the direction of community, Catholics often are motivated by the idea of "what's in it for me." People who joined the New Jerusalem Community realized in retrospect that they were more interested in how the community could benefit them rather than in how they could be a blessing to others. When their expectations were not met, they moved on and looked in other places to be satisfied.

The loss of community in Christianity is typified by the syndrome of TV evangelism. Television preachers proclaim a message of individual salvation which is tantamount to spiritual narcissism. They offer salvation to isolated individuals if, in the privacy of their own homes, they say that they believe in Jesus. These ministers show no awareness of salvation in and through the Church, no sense of the good news of the Kingdom. The great pity is that many people in the television audience are Catholics who have lost touch with the communal wisdom of their own tradition.

A Call to Social Transformation

Just as the call to personal conversion leads beyond the individual to community, so also the invitation to community ultimately leads beyond itself. Catholic wisdom is too aware of people's need for one another to be satisfied with individualistic piety and too aware of the Church's mission to be content with communal self-centeredness.

If living the gospel meant no more than forming a community, there would have been no reason for the Church to grow any larger than the small band of disciples who came to acknowledge Jesus as the Messiah. Christianity could have remained a small religious movement gathered around the apostles and their successors.

The apostles, however, realized that the good news that Jesus had revealed was meant not just for them but for the whole world. Through his preaching and his ministry Jesus proclaimed that his Father's incredible love extended to everyone, and through his death and resurrection Jesus made it possible for everyone to die and rise to new life. From the very beginning, then, the apostles saw that their purpose was to bring the gospel to the ends of the earth and to bring the whole world to Christ.

The mission of the Church is to complete what the apostles began. The Church is a sign of Christ's continued presence in the world. Just as the apostles proclaimed that Jesus was no longer dead but living and risen in their midst, the Church proclaims that Christ is alive and active in the world and celebrates this living reality in the Eucharist. Filled with the Spirit of God, the Church carries on the ministry of Jesus, announcing the unbounded love of God and caring for those who do not believe that anyone could care for them. It is a sacrament of Jesus in the world, and it commemorates that in the sacrament that signifies the communion that Jesus wants to have with everyone.

The Eucharist, however, is not just communion. The first part of the eucharistic liturgy is the proclamation of the word of God in the Scriptures. The Church is the place where the word of God is preserved and taught, in preparation for its being lived. Before the Bible as we know it was written, the Christian community was passing on the stories of Jesus and teaching others to live the way that Jesus made possible. In other words, the Church came before the Bible. The community mission created the community narratives.

The Eucharist does not end with communion but with our being told to "Go out to love and serve the Lord." We do this individually by loving and serving the community which is the Body of Christ. But we do this together, as a corporate body, by loving and serving Christ wherever he is found, even in "the least of my brethren" (Matthew 25:40). The mission of the Church is to carry the love and service of Jesus to all people, unto the ends of the earth and until the end of time.

The Church as Church, therefore, has a mission which extends beyond itself. Its mission is the extension of the Kingdom to all people and the transformation of the world into the Kingdom of God. For this reason, the Catholic tradition has always been one of social transformation, both the transformation of society within the Church and the transformation of society beyond the Church.

The Church itself is meant to be a transformed society, a place where God's love is experienced in community and celebrated in liturgy. It is to be a place where God's forgiveness is given to all and signified in sacrament. It is to be a place where the Lord's service is extended to all and acknowledged in ministry. It is to be a place where the Spirit's power is received by all and experienced in reformed lives and transformed relationships. The primary part of the Church's mission is to be itself, to be Church, to be what it is meant to be, and that includes service and love of those beyond the Church.

The Catholic Church has traditionally implemented this part of its mission through continuous self-renewal. Some

Catholics believe renewal began with the Second Vatican Council in the 1960's, but that council was the twenty-first in the Church's history. In fact, the majority of ecumenical councils have been called for the sake of reform and renewal.

Reform in the Church began as early as New Testament times. In chapter 15 of the Book of Acts we read that around A.D. 50, the apostles gathered in Jerusalem to discuss whether non-Jewish converts should have to follow Jewish dietary laws and other customs. The assembled leaders decided that for the good of the whole Church, those Jewish traditions would not be imposed on new Gentile converts. We also see in his letters that St. Paul tried constantly to reform the communities he founded, calling them to live the fullness of the gospel that he preached to them.

The Church was renewed by the monastic movement that began in the fourth century and by numerous monastic reforms in the centuries that followed. The ninth century ushered in a long period of medieval renewal that began with liturgical changes, continued through the revision of canon law and culminated in the development of scholastic theology in the 13th century. The Council of Trent in the 16th century was essentially a reform council, called to answer the challenge of the Protestant Reformation. The centuries that followed saw the rise of many religious orders still in the Church today. Each new religious order attempted to renew from within some aspect of the Church.

It is clear, then, that Catholic wisdom perceives the need for self-criticism and self-renewal. The Catholic tradition of growth in holiness calls not just individuals but the whole Church to conversion and transformation. Those who protest against changes brought about since Vatican II, insinuating that the Church has abandoned its tradition, obviously take a rather shortsighted view of tradition. They have in mind only the traditions of the past 400 years or so and overlook changes that actually occurred in the Church during the centuries following the Council of Trent. More importantly, they lose sight of the 2,000-year history of growth and renewal in the Church, which is the great tradition of Catholicism.

Such "traditionalists" are therefore really anti-traditionalists. They naively mistake Catholicism as they encountered it a few decades ago for Catholicism as it has existed for centuries. The famous English theologian, John Henry Newman, observed more than a hundred years ago, "To grow is to change, and to be perfect is to have changed often." When Cardinal Newman wrote those words, it was customary to refer to the Church as a "perfect society." Few people at the time were as conversant with Church history as Newman, and he saw clearly that the Church's ability to adapt and grow was integral to its perfection.

Catholicism's call for social transformation, however, extends beyond the boundaries of the Church itself. Western society has been transformed again and again by Christianity, and the Church has often (if not always) been active in that social transformation. Catholics have always been concerned for people's welfare.

In ancient Rome Church leaders protested against gladiator fights and other forms of killing for sport. Christians were forbidden to attend such "public games," and eventually the Church compelled the government to outlaw them. Church leaders also were instrumental in getting laws passed that protected the rights of widows and orphans, that curtailed slavery, that reduced abortions and that provided for the humane treatment of criminals.

In the Middle Ages the Church protected peasants against the tyranny of nobles. It gave sanctuary to people who broke unjust laws or who were wanted for protesting against harsh treatment and unfair taxation. It declared that the so-called divine right of kings was limited by God's law of justice, and it acted as a court of appeals for people who felt they had been wronged by civil courts. It proposed the "just war" theory to limit the atrocities of warfare, and it even declared a "truce of God" which forbade fighting on certain holy days.

Monasteries were the first hospitals for the sick and the first hotels for weary pilgrims. (Both "hospital" and "hotel" come from the same word, *hospes*, meaning one who shares hospitality.) Monasteries were also the first schools in the

Middle Ages, and the monks taught not only religion and the classics but also practical methods of engineering and farming. Men and women in religious orders, committed to being "in the world but not of the world," carried this tradition of caring for people's welfare beyond the monasteries and into society at large. One religious order, the Mercedarians, dedicated itself to ransoming Christian slaves from non-Christian pirates and rulers, going so far as to offer themselves in exchange when they could not buy the captured person's freedom.

In modern times missionaries have fought against the enslavement of Africans and Indians in agrarian societies. Popes Leo XIII and Pius XI both wrote encyclicals denouncing the dehumanization of factory workers in industrial societies. Popes John XXIII and Paul VI called for a more equitable distribution of the world's wealth between rich and poor nations. Pope John Paul II likewise has called for the humanization of the workplace and the Christianization of the marketplace. American bishops continue to protest against the exploitation of migrant laborers, to call public attention to the plight of farm families, to support the homeless and persons with AIDS, and to condemn the arms race and use of nuclear weapons.

On the other side exist Catholics who believe the Church should stay out of society's business. They want Church leaders to stick to "religion" and say nothing about economics and politics. They claim that Catholicism should be concerned only with the welfare of souls and not with the well-being of people in society.

Such Catholics, however, like those who protest against changes within the Church, have lost contact with the Catholic tradition of social transformation. They do not have the holistic vision of Catholicism; they see the sacred and the secular as separate realms. They do not remember that the Church has always been concerned with how people are treated and how they treat one another. They forget that an integral part of the Church's mission is to bring about, as far as possible, the realization of God's Kingdom on earth.

The Church's concern for human welfare, and in

particular for the welfare of the poor and underprivileged, springs directly from the Catholic understanding of holistic growth and universal salvation. God wants everyone to reach their full potential, to be as whole and as holy as possible. First, this means having basic human needs met so that people are free from physical want and emotional distress. Second, it means fulfilling the spiritual dimension of their personality, growing to full maturity in Christ through their relationship with God and through meeting the needs of others. The gospel is a message to be shared at every level of human life, physical and emotional as well as spiritual. Christianity is a way of life to be embraced by individuals, communities and societies. The good news is that God's power, the power of the Holy Spirit, is available for both the salvation of souls and the redemption of the world.

Accepting the Catholic vision means never accepting things the way they are. People always hurt and suffer oppression. People always need to be healed and set free. But to stop much of the pain and hurt, society itself has to be transformed. Being Catholic means taking one's place in the long tradition of those Christian social reformers who have always wanted to change the world, making it more like God's Kingdom.

A Profound Sense of History

Catholic consciousness is a historical consciousness. Participating in the Catholic tradition means being aware that our Church has been in existence for a long time and that our Judeo-Christian heritage stretches back even farther in time.

The Catholic Church has made its presence felt and been influenced by Western culture for nearly 20 centuries—four or five times the age of the oldest Protestant denomination and 10 times as old as the United States. Belonging to a Church with that lengthy history gives Catholics a unique historical perspective.

At least, it should. Too often we as Americans live in the

immediacy of the present. We forget that most of the problems we face today as individuals and as a society have been addressed by the Church century after century. The solution to many individual problems (usually referred to as personal sins) is to live the gospel in community. The solution to many social problems (often referred to as social evils) is to share the gospel with the world.

How quickly we Americans forget that the English once were our enemies, as were the Germans and the Japanese even more recently. How completely we forget the conversion of Russia some 10 centuries ago and that the majority of people who live under communism are Christians. When we forget that most people who would be killed by our nuclear attack are our sisters and brothers in Christ, it is easy to picture them as our enemies. Yet our history shows that those who were once considered enemies can become friends.

In its 2,000 years the Church has lived under kings and emperors, in democracies and dictatorships, with capitalism and communism. The Catholic perspective on history shows that we do not have to fear any political or economic system. The gospel of Jesus can be lived in any place, at any time, under any conditions. In historical fact Christianity has sometimes flourished most during periods of religious persecution.

If we stay connected to our Catholic past, we understand that war solves only immediate problems and always causes new ones. In the long run the only wise solution is the risk of peace, not peace such as the world gives by force of arms, but peace that comes from daring to love, as Jesus did, even our enemies.

A Catholic humorist once observed, "We have to love our enemies—including pastors, too!" In any community or institution the people we hate the most often are the ones in charge, rather than people outside the group. In the Church we often harbor a uniquely intense anger towards the clergy or religious. Sometimes this anger may be personal, for what they have done to deliberately offend or slight us. Frequently, though, the anger is directed against an individual that we have never met, or against authority in general, for doing or failing to do something in the Church.

When our anger rises in response to changes in the Church (whether we believe the changes are too fast and too many or too slow and too few), it could be because we look at the immediate situation rather than take a historical overview. The Catholic consciousness of history is so immensely long that much of what happens (or fails to happen) in the Church can only be understood within a historical perspective.

We have seen already that those who are disturbed by recent changes in the Church do not appreciate the full Catholic tradition of institutional development and social involvement. Those bothered by the failure of the Church to change itself or the world fast enough, however, likewise do not appreciate the full history of the Catholic tradition. It is, after all, a very long tradition, one that has seen many changes.

Whereas we as individuals tend to look at change in terms of the years within our lifetime, the Church as an institution tends to look at change in terms of centuries. Most of the Church leaders in Rome, for example, think of change as occuring slowly over the course of generations, for the major changes in the Church's history always have taken a long time. They see the slow evolution, for example, from adult to infant baptism, from married to celibate clergy, from informal to formal celebrations of the sacraments, and from few to many marriage laws, and so they are puzzled by the demand from some quarters that the reverse changes should take place immediately. They are quite content to continue to let things evolve slowly, under the guidance of the Holy Spirit, and to make institutional changes only when unavoidable.

This does not imply that no institutional inertia exists in the Church or no personal stubbornness in its leaders—far from it! But it suggests that not all resistance to change is the result of malicious or morbid rigidity. Often enough, Church leaders refuse to make changes immediately because they see changes coming inevitably, when perhaps there will be less negative reaction.

This slowness to change causes suffering among those who see the immediate good that would result from changes, such as allowing laicized priests to return to active ministry, encouraging laypeople to assume leadership roles and decentralizing the authority of the hierarchy. Such suffering is unfortunate. It is painful for many people of goodwill in the Church; they see the fruits of such possible changes withering before their eyes, dying on the vine. They can almost taste how good it would be for the Church—and for themselves personally—if Rome would make these changes right away.

The Catholic consciousness of history does not take away the suffering, but it alleviates the pain. A profound sense of history makes us aware that change for the better has already occurred and so it keeps alive the hope that good changes will continue. It gives us an awareness that the Spirit is indeed moving in the Church, a movement always toward fuller life and freedom. It suggests we focus on changes that are in fact occurring, instead of bemoaning changes that have not yet occurred.

Perhaps we could say that a special virtue, a virtue of Catholic patience, comes from fully appreciating the longevity of the Catholic tradition. It takes the edge off our impatience with the institution and the steam out of our anger with its leaders. It enables us to look at the Church from a perspective closer to the way that God must look at human history and with a sort of divine patience. And it gives us the wisdom to cooperate with the Spirit, doing what we can in the Body of Christ, while leaving the rest in God's hands.

An Optimistic Attitude

All characteristics of Catholicism treated in this chapter spring from an underlying attitude of optimism about life, human nature and history. A truly Catholic consciousness looks at the world, which obviously contains both good and bad, and focuses on the good. Catholicism looks at people and emphasizes the goodness in them and their potential for even greater goodness. It looks at the ups and downs of history and insists that progress outweighs decline.

Such optimism is not characteristic of all religious traditions. Dualistic religions divide reality into matter and spirit, and they assert that only the spiritual world is truly good and the material world is basically evil. The Calvinistic tradition in Protestantism considers human nature to be so corrupt that even the best of people are base sinners. Eastern religions, such as Hinduism and Buddhism, regard history as an illusion that hides a revolving time of eternally recurring sameness.

Catholicism admits the reality of sin and evil, but it does not start there. It begins with the goodness of creation and proposes that evil can be measured only as a lack of perfect goodness, as the necessary imperfection of a world that is not God. It begins with the original goodness of human nature and suggests that sin is an aftereffect of human freedom, a consequence of choosing that has gone astray. It begins with an evolutionary conception of history, beginning with the creation of the world by God and adding revelation after revelation about human destiny, without denying that at times the more things change the more they seem to remain the same.

This optimistic attitude pervades all Catholic philosophy, theology and morality. Philosophically, Catholicism believes that the human being has an infinite potential for development. It suggests that we can and do know God, even if only inadequately, and that our intellectual yearning for knowledge will be satisfied when we see God face to face. It assumes that since we are made in the spiritual likeness of God, we can and ought to strive to comprehend everything that God has made, seeking the divine unity of it all. It declares that even the humblest of persons should aspire to the heights of sanctity and the fulfillment of human potential.

Theologically, Catholicism begins with the unity of all in God and only afterwards does it draw distinctions between the divine and the human. The Catholic religious imagination sees God shining through the universe, revealing the truly infinite in the not-quite infinite. It perceives the fundamental unity of all people, calling them the children of a common God. It asserts that in Jesus the divine and the human were completely united and that in the Eucharist that same Jesus is completely present. It looks at the visible world and sees sacraments of God everywhere, in bread and wine, water and oil, fire and wind, smoke and ashes, touch and even sex. It assumes that God's love is found in the midst of human love, that divine justice is at the core of human justice, that the life of the Trinity is at the heart of life-giving human relationships.

Morally, Catholicism emphasizes God's initiative rather than the human response. It looks at morality from the divine perspective of love and forgiveness rather than from the human perspective of sin and failure. Sometimes it has gone too far in this direction, giving the impression that people can do anything they want as long as they go to confession afterwards. Sometimes it has been overly optimistic, suggesting that the poor will get their reward in heaven, allowing the rich to escape examining their conscience about social sin.

Other Christian denominations which emphasize the human response can put Catholics to shame with their moral rigor. They insist on the literal observance of the Ten Commandments, on clean living without gambling, drinking or smoking, on supporting their ministries through tithing, on maintaining the integrity of family life, on working to bring the world to Christ. Catholic morality has tended to be lax except in the area of sexuality, where for cultural reasons it has been scrupulously rigorous.

Although the Catholic Church has tended to overlook its own moral shortcomings, its broader vision of morality is still fundamentally scriptural. The Judeo-Christian Bible reveals a God who is gracious and forgiving and understanding. The Scriptures speak eloquently of God's unconditional love for people despite their moral failing and of God's constant forgiveness of people who admit their weakness.

Protestants are often fond of quoting John 3:16 to prove that God took the initiative in the drama of salvation: "God so loved the world that he gave his only begotten Son, that whosoever believes in him should not perish but have everlasting life." They may even cite Ephesians 2:4-5 to emphasize their point: "God is rich in mercy, and out of his great love for us, he brought us to life with Christ even when we were dead with sin. By grace have you been saved." Yet these quotations are but two of hundreds that underlie the Catholic understanding that morality begins and ends with acknowledging our complete dependence on God.

It has been said that Catholicism tends to produce a few spiritual giants and that Protestantism tends to produce many spiritual midgets. Although that is an oversimplification, you can see the truth to it. The Protestant churches know how to get people involved in Bible study, shared prayer and communal worship so that many individuals come to know the Lord and live according to God's word. All too often, however, Protestants take the beginning of spiritual growth as the be-all and end-all of Christian life. They get stuck at the starting point of developing a personal relationship with Christ (which is basic, to be sure) and never get beyond the basics of conversion, morality and prayer.

The Catholic Church is where you have to look to find Christians who are larger than life. Individuals like Augustine and Aquinas, Catherine of Siena and Teresa of Avila, Francis of Assisi and Mother Teresa of Calcutta are truly heroic figures. Their religious discipline led them to such heights of spiritual development and depths of personal integration that they arouse our admiration. They are the really whole and holy people in the Christian tradition. They are the people who are pointed to as saints. By and large, they come out of the Catholic Church.

Unfortunately, however, most Catholics do not get that far. They do not even try to get that far. They just stand back and point to the spiritual giants in Catholicism as if the saints validated the moral life of the entire Catholic Church. Most Catholics never experience personal conversion; they never get beyond rote prayer; they never read the Bible; they never grow past legalistic morality. They never even become spiritual midgets.

It is sad, but in many ways the institutional Church has been the source of this paradox. The Church kept alive the great Catholic tradition, but it often kept the secret of its vitality hidden from all but the privileged few who entered monasteries and religious orders. It frequently misjudged the saints in their own day (just as institutional Judaism persecuted the prophets of Israel), only to glorify them afterwards. The masses of Catholics in medieval and modern times were led to believe that the saints were incredible exceptions rather than examples of what they could aspire to. Church leaders all too often were content to feed the people crumbs instead of inviting them to feast at the banquet of God's Kingdom. Perhaps if the medieval Church had been living up to its mission, the Protestant Reformation would not have been called for. Perhaps if the modern Church had been living up to its vision of unity, Europe would have been spared countless religious wars and two global conflicts started mainly by Christians and ex-Christians.

The failures of Catholicism as an institution point to a darker side of the Church's history. The Catholic appreciation for creation has sometimes overemphasized "the good life" for those in power and disregarded the needs of the poor. In recent centuries the Catholic Church has been rather provincial, narrowly insisting on European and Italian ways of doing things. At times, the Church has demanded legalistic obedience instead of personal holiness, and it has stood for the status quo rather than social transformation. It often has mistaken conformity for community and suppressed individuality. The Church also has been forgetful of its own history, sometimes substituting shallow traditions for its much deeper wisdom tradition. And Catholicism has suffered from its own brands of fundamentalism and anti-intellectual dogmatism.

To be honest with ourselves and truthful to our critics we must acknowledge that, for all its brilliance, Catholicism casts a dark shadow. To the exploration of that shadow we must now turn. The challenge of being Catholic is to know both the good and the bad about the Church, but also to affirm the good in order to build on the best in our tradition.

Chapter Two

What Is the Shadow Side of Catholicism?

The greater the light, the darker the shadow it casts. That is true of any source of light, whether we speak literally or metaphorically. The sun's shadow on the dark side of the moon is absolutely black; the shadow cast by a candle in a room is much softer. A good person radiates light into the lives of those around. Great and influential people are bright lights in history: They do much good, but they also can do much harm. The same is true of great institutions, such as the Catholic Church.

When we speak of the shadow side of a person or an institution, we speak in terms of Jungian psychology. According to psychologist Carl Jung, every person has a side of which he or she is conscious. It includes the person's positive attributes, the aspects of their personality they are aware of, perhaps even proud of. But every person also has a side of their personality that they are unaware of. It is hidden from their view in the darkness of their own unconscious. Often others are aware of these negative traits, but the individuals themselves do not notice them. A man can have a habit of cracking his knuckles, for example, without realizing that he is annoying others or even that he is cracking them at all. Or a woman can lose her temper with her children, believing that her outburst will make them behave. She does not see that her outburst also is making them hate her.

No one is perfect. We all have a shadow side of our

personality, and we all cast some darkness into the world around us. The same is true of groups, communities and institutions. Each has certain gifts or charisms that are a source of light. That is why people join groups: They are attracted by the light they see, and they want to benefit from the group's gifts. But no group is perfect, either. Sooner or later, those who join discover the group's shortcomings; they encounter its shadow. They may become discouraged, disillusioned, or even leave the group. Critics of any group, community or institution always criticize its darker side.

Just as the brightness of Catholicism comes from many sources, its darkness does also. The brightness of Catholicism comes, first of all, from Jesus, from the revelation that he was and from the gospel that he preached. The brightness also comes from the Jewish tradition that he was born into and from the Spirit that energized the early Church. It comes as well from the pastoral wisdom of its leaders, the holiness of it saints, the insight of its theologians and the faithfulness of its people through almost 2,000 years. The cumulative brightness of Catholicism is the culmination of its long and great tradition.

The darkness of Catholicism likewise comes from many sources. Jesus did not say everything that could be said about the gospel, and so Christians have sometimes misinterpreted his message. Both the Eastern and the Western cultures in which Christianity has flourished have their good sides, but they also have their shadows. Similarly, individuals and institutions in history have contributed parts of their own shadows to the collective darkness of the Church. The Church is not perfect today partly because of the shadows it has inherited.

In every person, in every group and even in every tradition, therefore, there is both light and dark, brightness and shadow. Chapter One said much about the brilliance of the Catholic tradition. It is time now to peer into its darkness.

Uncatholic Catholicism

The shadow is what a person is unaware of. It is by and large unconscious. Catholics often have a great sense of pride in their tradition, an awareness that their history goes back 20 centuries, a consciousness that theirs is a worldwide Church.

Strange to say, however, the sense of pride is often a cover-up for ignorance. Most Catholics today know that their Church has a great tradition, but they do not really know what that tradition is. They know they have a history, but they do not know their history. They know that the Church is in every country of the world, but they think that the Church is everywhere just like their own home parish. They are very parochial Catholics, very uncatholic Catholics.

Uncatholic Catholics have never been exposed to the great wisdom tradition of Catholicism. Whether this is due to the shortcomings of religious education today or whether it is due to other factors is beside the point. The slew of facts that bombard us every day can easily make the wisdom of Catholicism look like just more interesting information. The complexity of daily living can easily make the simplicity of the gospel look naive. For one reason or another, Catholics today are not seeking wisdom from the Scriptures, from the saints and mystics, from the philosophers and theologians who have contributed to the greatness of Catholicism. Instead of being large-souled persons they are small-minded individuals, as are many people in our world today.

Uncatholic Catholics are ignorant of the history of their tradition. Like most Americans, they are unhistorical in their thinking. If they have a sense of history, it is likely to be limited. They believe that the past was much like the present, or their knowledge of the past is very sketchy and selective. Their Catholic outlook is therefore not truly universal but rather limited. They think of themselves as part of a historical tradition, but their shadow is that they think unhistorically about it. At best, they are aware of recent traditions, but they mistake them for the great Catholic tradition.

Uncatholic Catholics are not community-minded. Like most people in the modern era, they are individualists. They think of themselves first and others second. They think of their parish or their city or their country first and others second. They do not act first and foremost out of a concern for the common good. When they do seek community, most often they are asking what is in it for themselves. They want the benefits of community without wanting to benefit the community. Yet they speak the language of community, extolling "the parish family," "the Church community," "the people of God." Their language hides the dark fact that most Catholics have an individualistic consciousness. They lead isolated lives, unconcerned about other people's loneliness.

These three elements in the shadow of contemporary Catholicism come largely from our Western heritage. Western culture, as we saw in Chapter One, is practical-minded rather than wisdom-minded. Western consciousness remembers the immediate past in order to manipulate the immediate future, and so it is not historically minded in either direction. Western society since the 16th century has been individualistic, and so it is neither community-minded nor ecology-minded.

The mistake we make when we take pragmatic, recent, individualistic religion as authentic is that we lose our own tradition. We call ourselves Catholics, yet we are not truly Catholic, truly universal in soul and spirit. Our critics can see that so well, yet we are blind to it. Our small-mindedness gives Catholicism a bad name, and our provincialism gives the Catholic Church a reputation it does not deserve. We do not really represent our own tradition, and so those outside cannot perceive its greatness. We do not really live our own tradition, and so even our children cannot see it. The tradition is in danger of being lost.

Ethnic Catholicism

A good deal of what passes for Catholicism is really a type of ethnic religiosity. As such, it is only nominally Catholic and nominally Christian. It is the religion of an ethnic group or nationality: Everyone who belongs to that ethnic group accepts that religion because they are born into it. They do not choose to be Catholic any more than they choose to be Italian or French, Spanish or Portuguese, Irish or German, Slovak or Polish, Mexican or Filipino, or any other nationality that is largely Catholic.

For many people and for many years, ethnic Catholicism was a good thing. If it did not have a lot of good in it, it would not have lasted as long as it did. When the people of Europe were converted to Christianity, the gospel was planted in many native soils. On the large scale, we can say that the soil in which Christianity took root was Western culture, and the religion that flourished was Western Christendom, or European Catholicism. Across Europe, however, there were in fact many variations of that Western culture. This was the variety of national cultures which, after the Middle Ages had passed, evolved into the modern nations that we know today.

When Christianity was first being introduced to these ethnic groupings of peoples, they of course understood the gospel as best they could. They were, as the Romans called them, barbarians. They were crude and illiterate. They were wild and uncivilized. They were often at war with one another. Christianity tamed their barbaric instincts. It gave them a higher standard of morality. It gave them a deeper purpose and a broader vision. Christianity unified Europe in the Middle Ages under a common religion and a common moral code.

As we might expect, the common people's understanding of the gospel was basic. They were impressed by the stories in the Old Testament—the stories about Adam and Eve, Noah and the flood, Moses and the burning bush, David and Goliath. They marveled at the stories in the New Testament— the stories about Jesus being born in a stable, his healing the sick and forgiving sinners, his walking on water and calming the storm, his bloody crucifixion and glorious resurrection. These biblical stories were illustrated again and again in the stained-glass windows of the great medieval cathedrals. The stories of salvation history became a part of their religious heritage.

41

The common people also expressed their understanding of the gospel in their own unique ethnic ways. In Italy the birth of Jesus was displayed in manger scenes. In Spain the suffering of Christ was dramatized in passion processions. In many parts of Europe the stories of the Bible were acted out in miracle plays. Local saints were remembered and honored on their feast days. Through celebrations such as these, the Judeo-Christian tradition was preserved in a variety of ethnic traditions, and it found expression in many different European cultures.

The reverse also happened. Ethnic customs were incorporated into Christianity. The Christmas tree and wreath were borrowed from the pagan winter festivals of northern Europe, and the Easter egg and rabbit were imported from the pagan spring rituals of southern and eastern Europe. These and other symbols were given Christian meanings, but they still retained their ethnic identity. People identified with Christianity in their own cultural ways.

In time the Christian tradition became so intertwined with cultural traditions that it was impossible to tell them apart. Christianity was mixed with cultural identity—or rather, with a number of cultural identities. Each national and ethnic group had their own unique ways of expressing and celebrating their faith. Each identified their own traditions with the Christian tradition. When they felt threatened as a people, they derived strength from their faith. When their country was attacked, they were confident that God was on their side. When they emigrated to foreign lands, they found unity in their Church.

This type of ethnic Christianity, however, also has a dark side. It is found in Protestantism as well as Catholicism, in British Anglicanism, in German Lutheranism, in South African Calvinism. It is found in Russian and Greek Orthodoxy, in Southern Baptists and in many fundamentalist churches. Ethnic Christianity is not unique to Catholicism, but it is as true of Catholicism as it is of any other denomination.

Ethnic Christianity casts three dark shadows on the world

in which we live. It is peripheral, it is self-righteous and it is ultimately nominal Christianity.

Ethnic religion, including the Catholic form of it, is more concerned with peripheral than central issues. It is taken up with traditions rather than being attentive to the great tradition. Its focus is more on external observance than on inner conversion. Much of the resistance to changes in the Church in the 1970's was fueled by worry about the loss of many of the visible trappings of Catholicism—statues in churches, novenas and devotions, St. Christopher medals and the like. At the same time, much of the rejoicing about the same changes came from the belief that the Church needed a more modern look—perhaps even a more "American" look.

Many thought that the external changes signalled deeper changes in the spiritual life of American Catholics. In fact, however, those deeper changes did not occur, at least not on a wide scale.

We can see this in contrasting ways in both the laity and the hierarchy. The American bishops and Pope John Paul II in the 1980's called for changes in military and economic policy, yet the Catholic laity have by and large ignored them. Laypeople on the other hand have asked for changes in the authority structure of the Church, yet the hierarchy have for the most part resisted. It is much easier to manipulate the externals of Catholicism than to convert hearts and minds. Yet conversion is a central issue in Christianity. Conversion—from war-making to peace-making, from consuming to sharing, from dictating to cooperating—is what the gospel of Jesus is all about.

Ethnic Catholicism can stubbornly resist conversion because it is self-righteous. Not long ago in our own country French and German Catholics disdained Irish Catholics, who in turn wanted nothing to do with Italian Catholics and other immigrants from southern and eastern Europe. When Catholics gained local political power in America, as various ethnic groups did in the cities where they concentrated, they often used that power to their own advantage in very unchristian ways. Today in countries where Catholics are in the majority, as in Latin America, the ethnic Church often preserves its privileged position and pious practices while ignoring the gross injustices around it.

Like nationalism, ethnic Christianity justifies itself by identifying itself with those in power. When those in power are the majority, this is especially easy to do. The majority look at things in a certain way, and since very few object it seems as though their view is obviously correct. The majority can make decisions that are favorable to themselves, and even though those decisions might hurt a minority, the majority can overrule them. As a result, the majority view is never seriously questioned. It appears to be so right, so fair, so just. It is justified by the simple fact that everyone seems to believe it. It is self-justifying and self-righteous.

In reality the majority view can be very unfair and very unjust. It can perpetuate racial, religious, sex and age discrimination. It can condone unfair labor practices and unjust trade agreements. It can refuse to make changes that would enable those who are not in power to get a better education, decent housing, needed jobs and minimal health care. Yet because the majority are not concerned about these things, nothing is done about them.

When the majority are Christians, the majority view seems to be the Christian view. Because it is self-justifying, no one asks whether it is really Christ's view. Because it is self-righteous, no one asks whether it is really right according to the standards of the gospel. The gospel is identified with culture and society, whereas in reality the gospel is very countercultural. In cultural Christianity and ethnic Catholicism the gospel is not seen for what it really is, and so people do not live according to the teachings of Jesus. They live according to the standards of society, yet they call it Christian.

Consequently, ethnic Catholicism is only nominally Christian. People are Catholics by birth yet Christians in name only. They call themselves Catholics, yet they do not live up to their Christian calling. They belong to the Catholic Church, yet they do not really follow Jesus. Jesus forgave sinners, but they want severe punishment for criminals.

Jesus said love your enemies, but they want more sophisticated weapons. Jesus proclaimed the Kingdom of God, but they preach national self-interest. Jesus said it is blessed to be poor, but they want to be happily rich. The contrasts between the gospel of Jesus and the way most Catholics live could be multiplied indefinitely.

To be honest, though, the fault does not lie with individual Catholics. It lies with ethnic Catholicism. Most Catholics are good people who are trying to be Christian. The ethnic Church in which they were brought up, however, taught them Catholic traditions rather than the Judeo-Christian tradition. It taught them religion rather than the gospel. It told them to go to Mass on Sunday rather than to form community. It told them to listen to the clergy rather than to read the Scriptures. It told them to obey the Commandments rather than to live the Beatitudes. It told them to worry about sexual sins rather than to question the evils of wealth and power.

There is a famous story in Dostoevsky's novel, *The Brothers Karamazov*. Jesus returns to earth during the Middle Ages, only to be arrested by the Grand Inquisitor and summoned for questioning. He is accused of leading people astray by telling them that love is more important than obedience, that forgiveness is more important than going to confession, that the Kingdom of God is more important than the Church. The Inquisitor shrewdly guesses who the man before him really is, but he does not want him upsetting the ethnic Catholicism of medieval Spain. In the end he threatens Christ with execution if he does not leave the Church alone.

One wonders whether Jesus might receive similar treatment today if he returned and questioned the ethnic Catholicism in modern America.

Institutional Catholicism

If there is one word that characterizes the Catholic Church, it is *institution*. Each of our parishes is an institution in itself, with administration and staff, programs and budgets, buildings and grounds. Catholic institutions abound: schools and seminaries, hospitals and social agencies, monasteries and retreat houses. The organization of the Catholic Church is highly institutionalized, from the Vatican with its worldwide secretariats, to the diocese with its many offices, to the religious order with its many provinces.

There is a positive side to institutionalization. If you want to do something only once, you only have to do it. If you want to do something over and over again, though, you have to institutionalize it in some way. You have to institute some program that will ensure that the job gets done not just today or this year but also tomorrow and next year and the year after that. Human life would be chaotic were it not for institutions. It would be like having to reinvent the wheel day in and day out.

Christianity developed institutions very early in its history. At the beginning, the apostles had no set plan of action. They rushed out of the upper room on Pentecost and began to preach, proclaiming Jesus as the messiah and calling people to conversion. They baptized people and formed communities, meeting in houses to share the Lord's Supper, praying in synagogues or wherever else they would be allowed to gather. Missionaries like St. Paul went off in all directions to spread the word about Jesus and the coming of God's Kingdom.

Quickly, however, community life developed certain rhythms and structures. Christians met regularly on the first day of the week, Sunday, to celebrate the Resurrection and thank God for sending Jesus. Men and women were appointed to take care of the poor, the widowed and the orphaned. Elders were selected to supervise local communities, preside at worship and preserve the teaching of the apostles. We can read about these developments even in the New Testament, in the Acts of the Apostles and in many of the Epistles. The Church was instituting what needed to be done to serve the needs of the community and to bring the gospel to the world.

In time the institution of community life and missionary

activity succeeded in converting the whole known world at the time, the Roman Empire. When the Roman Empire fell to the barbarian invasions, its governmental institutions ceased to exist. The only institutions left were Church institutions: parishes, dioceses and monasteries. These institutions preserved what was left of Roman civilization and Western culture, besides preserving the gospel message and the Judeo-Christian tradition. The Church civilized and Christianized the barbaric tribes of Europe through its institutions, and gradually a new culture arose, that of medieval Christendom.

Were it not for Christian institutions and the institution of the Roman Church itself, history and the world today would be very different. The Church as an institution has been a positive influence for millions of people and for centuries.

But there is also a negative aspect to institutionalization. Institutions take on a life of their own. They are self-perpetuating and difficult to change. They set up structures that are stronger than the individuals who function within them. Yet their very strength is also their weakness. Their bright side also has a dark side.

The institutional structures of Roman Catholicism, as we have already noted in Chapter One, are culturally Western. That is, they are hierarchical and authoritarian. They are organizational pyramids. Orders come from the top and filter through a series of levels, until they reach the bottom. Society is divided into the leaders and the led, the teachers and the taught. Church society is divided into the shepherds and the sheep, the clergy and the laity.

The strength of this institutional structure is its ability to establish and maintain communities and organizations. When people respect authority, they are willing to subordinate their individual desires for the good of the whole. Too often, however, people in religious institutions subordinate their intelligence and initiative to the will of those at the top of the hierarchical ladder, and they become powerless and passive. They do not do anything that they do not have to do. They let others do their thinking for them. They are satisfied with minimum morality instead of striving for maximum goodness.

There is a place for leadership in the Church. There is a passage in Luke's Gospel where Jesus foretells that Peter is going to deny him, and Jesus tells Peter what he wants him to do afterwards:

> Simon, Simon! Satan wants to test you, to shake
> you as the farmer shakes wheat to sift the grain
> from the chaff. But I have prayed for you that your
> faith will not fail. When you have turned back to
> me, you must turn to your brothers and
> strengthen them (Luke 22:31-32).

The role of leadership in the Church is to strengthen the members of the Church. Too often in the past, however, the leaders in the Church have weakened the people in the Church. They have identified their own faith with the faith of the institution, and they have told the people simply to believe what the institution says: to pray, pay and obey. The people obeyed, but they did not develop a mature faith of their own.

That is the weakness of a strong institution. The Church has maintained and perpetuated itself in a strongly authoritarian manner, giving people a sense of strength in size and numbers and stability. It did not, however, give them spiritual strength. It did not invite them to the experience of God, nor did it call them to a personal relationship with Jesus. It did not demand that they become disciples of Christ and followers of the gospel, only followers of the clergy. It did not give them a moral vision that went much beyond keeping the Commandments and avoiding sexual impurity. It did not suggest that they should take personal responsibility for their own moral decisions or adult responsibility for shaping the world into God's Kingdom. Under this paternalistic dominance, most Catholics' religious faith and moral conscience remained passively childish.

As a result, today we have a crisis of faith and a crisis of morality in the Church. The hierarchy in its authoritarian way tells people what to believe and how to behave, but many

Catholics resist. Sometimes it is because they are educated and they believe they should have some input into decisions that are made in the Church, whether those decisions come from the rectory, the chancery or the Vatican. Sometimes, though, it is because they want the hierarchy to tell them what to do, but the hierarchy does not say what they want to hear. In either case, they feel alienated, angry and abandoned. The crisis is also a crisis of authority.

There is a place for authority in the Church. There is a passage in Matthew's Gospel which always has been very dear to Catholics because it affirms the faith and the authority of Peter, the first among the Apostles. After Peter professes his belief that Jesus is the Christ, Jesus turns to him and says:

> Good for you, Simon son of John! For no human
> being told you this, but it was revealed to you by
> my Father in heaven. Your name Peter means
> rock, and so you are. On this rock I will build my
> church, and not even the gates of hell will be able
> to stand up against it (Matthew 16:17-18).

The role of authority in the Church is to be a foundation on which community is built. It is to be a unified base from which the people of the Church move out into the world with Jesus' assurance that nothing can withstand the spread of the gospel. Jesus does not tell Peter that he *is* the Church, only that he is to give unity and stability to the Church. Too often in the past, however, the Church has been identified with the pope and the hierarchy. The clergy did everything in the Church, and the people did nothing. They were weak and passive. The hierarchy assumed authority in the Church and left the people powerless.

Again, as a result, we have a crisis of authority in the Church. The clergy once did everything for the people, but now when there are fewer priests to minister in parishes and hospitals, many people feel abandoned and lost. The clergy once seemed perfect, but now when people learn that some priests have drinking or sexual problems, many people feel angry and betrayed. They have put the clergy on a pedestal for so long that they do not know what to do when they discover that priests are just as human as they are. They have been ministered to for so long that they do not know how to minister to one another and the priests in their midst. The crisis is also a crisis of ministry.

In the end the crisis of authority *in* the Church becomes a crisis of the authority *of* the Church. The Church as a community of disciples is called to be a presence of Christ in the world, a light set upon a hill, a lamp shining in the darkness. When authority in the Church becomes restricted to the clergy, however, the authority of the whole body of believers in the world becomes diminished. The pope and the bishops speak, but the non-Catholic world does not have to listen, for the hierarchy are a tiny few. Even Catholics often do not listen, whether they agree and think that if the hierarchy speaks they themselves can passively do nothing, or whether they disagree and realize that the hierarchy cannot compel them.

When authority in the Church is institutionalized the way it has been since the Roman Empire, it has the strength of stability and longevity, but it also has the weakness of a ruling elite. As long as people were powerless, the power of the clergy often acted in their favor. Church institutions, manned by priests and monks, served the needs of the poor and the sick, the helpless and the uneducated. But pyramidal power from the top down also institutionalized passivity in the recipients of the clergy's ministry. Thus the bright side also had a dark side.

Today we see the dark side in the Catholic tendency to identify the Church with its institutions, or even with its clergy. Catholics do not think of themselves as the Church. They do not hear the words of Christ as addressed to them but to priests and nuns. They do not take responsibility for the Church's mission in the world, but they leave it instead to increasingly powerless Church institutions.

Unscriptural Catholicism

With few exceptions Catholics are not great readers of the Bible. Unlike Protestants (especially those who belong to evangelical or pentecostal denominations), Catholics tend to rely on the sacraments and teachings of the Church for their religious formation and knowledge of their faith.

There are two historical reasons for this state of affairs. The first is that the Church existed long before the Bible was completed and so came to rely much more on the spoken word than on the written word. Although early converts from Judaism accepted the Hebrew Scriptures (what we call today the Old Testament) as inspired by God, by the end of the first century the majority of Christians were converts from paganism who had known nothing about the Jewish religion and its sacred writings. During the second and third centuries there was even a debate in the Church about whether Christians should accept the Hebrew Scriptures as their own.

In addition to this we must remember that during the first century the Gospels and Epistles (which were eventually included in the New Testament) were still being written. These books were originally written for specific communities (for example, the Epistle to the Galatians), and although they began to be circulated around the Church during the second and third centuries, there was no authoritative list stating which writings should be accepted by all Christians.

It was not until the fourth century, therefore, when Christianity ceased to be an underground movement and the Church was given legal status, that bishops from around the Roman Empire could gather to decide on an official list or "canon" of the Scriptures. By this time it had already become customary for people to hear about Jesus by word of mouth, to be initiated into the Church through sacramental rites and to grow in their understanding of their faith by participating in the Sunday liturgy and listening to sermons. The Church's dependence on the oral transmission of the faith was reinforced by the fact that books had to be written out by hand on parchment or papyrus, so they were expensive and not readily available.

The second reason why Catholicism never depended strongly on the written word is that in the Middle Ages the vast majority of people in Europe were illiterate. By and large, only scholars and clerics knew how to read, and so the common people were instructed in their faith when they attended Mass and received the sacraments. If they were fortunate enough to live in a city, people could also learn the stories of the Bible from the stained-glass windows of the cathedral or by attending the miracle plays in the public square.

Protestants have sometimes accused the Catholic Church of not making the Scriptures readily available to the common people, and even of locking up or chaining Bibles in monasteries. When we recall, however, that producing a handwritten Bible in the Middle Ages took perhaps 500 parchment skins and 10,000 hours of manual labor, we can readily understand why Bibles were scarce and had to be protected against theft. The printing press was not invented until the middle of the 15th century, but the handmade Gutenberg Bible was still fairly expensive. The Protestant reformers could not have emphasized the reading of the Bible as much as they did were it not for the fact that by the 16th century books were becoming more plentiful and literacy was increasing.

We can easily see, therefore, why Catholicism never developed a tradition of encouraging individuals to read the Bible. After the Reformation, the Church shied away from telling people to read the Scriptures because Protestants used the Bible to argue against one another as well as against Rome, a practice that helped create the numerous denominations that exist today. For many centuries, individual interpretation of the Scriptures led to bitter division in Christianity.

Regardless of historical reasons, however, few Catholics do read the Bible, even in an age when almost everybody reads something every day. They do not use the Scriptures to increase their understanding of their religious tradition or to deepen their relationship with God. For many Catholics the Word of God is less authoritative than a teaching from the pope or a statement from their bishop or pastor. It is as though the Bible is unimportant unless it is backed up by the authority of a priest. This certainly is not a bright side of Catholicism.

The dark side of Protestantism, of course, is that it sometimes turns the Bible into a weapon of its own dogmatism. Fundamentalists often pride themselves on not believing in the authority of the pope, yet they can turn the Bible into a paper pope. Concealing that they are giving what amounts to their own interpretation of the Scriptures, evangelical preachers can use selected passages to prove a point and denounce anyone who opposes them. Hiding behind the authority of the Bible, they can be just as authoritarian as any Roman cleric.

On the brighter side, Protestants often read the Bible to guide their daily living. They engage in weekly Bible study or meditate on Scripture to increase their understanding of their faith and derive lessons on how to be better Christians. They look for lessons in the Bible on how to be good parents, honest business people and friendly neighbors.

The difference between scriptural Protestantism and unscriptural Catholicism is most obvious in traditionally Catholic countries when Protestant missionaries begin to arrive. The evangelical Christianity that they preach is quite a contrast to ethnic Catholicism. Mexico, for example, has been predominantly Catholic since its conquest by Spain, and in the 1950's Protestants were still rather rare. Around that same time, an anthropologist named Oscar Lewis lived among the poor in Mexico and wrote a book based on what they told him about their lives. In *Children of Sanchez: Autobiography of A Mexican Family*, Lewis tells the story of one young man he interviewed, named Manuel, who had been a Catholic all his life. Manuel described his situation this way:

> Well, I began analyzing things, right? Jesus said,
> "Like this fig tree, by their fruits you shall know

them." In the Mexican penitentiaries, out of one
hundred prisoners, ninety-nine are Catholics!
And if my friends who were thieves could light a
candle to a little saint before going out to rob, if
prostitutes kept a saint in their rooms, and burned
sanctified candles and prayed for more clients, if
there were such perversions within Catholicism,
well, can that be the true religion?...

Then I began to think about the Evangelists,
the Adventists, the Anglicans I knew. Well, I
never have seen one of them stretched out drunk
in the street, they never carried knives, or
smoked, took drugs, or cursed. Their homes had
everything they needed; their children were well
dressed and well fed, and they treated their wives
the way human beings should be treated. They
lived healthful and peaceful lives. But under
Catholicism, people live, well, the way I did.

I didn't lose my faith. I remained a Catholic,
because I didn't feel strong enough to obey the
commandments and to carry out the strict rules of
the Evangelists. I would no longer be able to
enjoy smoking, or gambling, or fornicating, and
well, I was absolutely incapable of living up to the
laws of God.

Manuel's words vividly portray the worst results of ethnic,
institutional, unscriptural Catholicism. In Chapter One we
saw that a bright side of the Catholic tradition was the
appreciation of creation, but here we see its corresponding
shadow. The optimistic attitude that we ought to enjoy the
good things in life can lead to an immoral neglect of Christian
values. The sacramental vision of the world as a revelation of
God can lead to a forgetfulness of God's revelation in the
Scriptures.

Unscriptural Catholicism was made possible by
sacramental Catholicism. For 15 centuries the sacraments
were absolutely necessary for introducing people to the
basics of Christianity, and in many ways they are still
essential to the Church's life. Just as the Bible can be used
wrongly, however, so too can the sacraments. They can
become rote rituals and mechanical dispensers of grace.

They can become substitutes for living according to the message of the gospel. They can give people a false sense of religious security and enable them to avoid any real moral conversion. They can lull people into liturgical lethargy rather than lead them to an encounter with God, as they are supposed to do.

In a Church that is authentically sacramental, the lessons of the Bible and the lessons of the sacraments are essentially the same, for the Scriptures are at the heart of liturgical worship. We see this most clearly in the Mass, where the Scriptures are read and explained and where the eucharistic action recalls Christ's Last Supper with the apostles. The same apostolic teaching that led to the writing of the New Testament led to the institution of the sacraments.

When the Church is inauthentically sacramental, however, it also becomes inauthentically scriptural. The same absentmindedness that leads to the mechanical performance of the sacraments leads to a forgetfulness of the Scriptures. The same religiosity that is comfortable with ritualism is happy to do without the Word of God, even when the Bible is readily available. Unscriptural Catholicism should therefore not be blamed on the sacraments but on their misunderstanding and misuse.

Undemanding Catholicism

The Catholic tradition is fundamentally a feminine tradition. That may sound odd, but in terms of religious attitude and outlook, Catholicism is much more feminine than masculine. The femininity of the Catholic Church turns up in the strangest places, in clerical dress and liturgical vestments, for example. Ours is one of the few churches where men dress in watered silk and lace when they want to look official and put on elaborate robes and fancy hats when they perform public duties. In solemn pronouncements about the Church they refer to it in Latin as *Sancta Mater Ecclesia*, "our Holy Mother the Church."

The femininity of Catholicism also shows up in our

devotion to Mary. Mary is honored not only as the Mother of Christ but also as the Mother of the Church. She is the refuge of the weak, the help of all Christians. Half of Europe's cathedrals are dedicated to her, and her title has always been *Our* Lady. She is the great mother symbol in the Catholic tradition, the symbol of the feminine dimension of God.

Protestantism, by and large, rejected devotion to Mary, although it continued to respect her as the mother of Jesus. It also eliminated the beautiful pageantry of medieval worship and the rich embellishment of church interiors. It substituted a much simpler style of worship and a much plainer church decor and did away with clerical dress. Protestantism represents a much more masculine view of life and approach to Christianity.

Catholicism, of course, also has its masculine element. Regardless of how they dress, men make the rules in the Catholic Church. One would hope that the masculine and feminine aspects of Catholicism would produce a holistic balance in the Church, but historically the masculine has dominated in structures of authority. As we saw in Chapter One, the Church organized itself according to the blueprint of Western culture, which was predominantly patriarchal and hierarchical. The Eastern side of Christianity, the matriarchal and feminine side, was preserved mainly in the Church's spirituality and liturgy. As we shall see shortly, Catholic morality also has been largely feminine in attitude and behavior.

If we compare masculine and feminine consciousness according to Jungian psychology, they can be defined in terms of contrasts. These contrasts are stereotypical or, more properly speaking, archetypal. They represent the *anima* or feminine soul and the *animus* or masculine soul. They do not dictate how women always look at things or how men always behave, but they are general tendencies in the attitudes and actions of most women and men. They are archetypes or general patterns of feeling and perception, outlook and behavior. In the typical woman the *anima* is conscious and dominant. She thinks and feels and behaves consciously like a woman. She also has an *animus*, however, which is largely unconscious but which enables her to develop the masculine dimension of her total personality. In the typical man, on the other hand, the *animus* is the conscious and dominant part of his soul. Yet he too has an unconscious *anima* which enables him to develop the feminine dimension of his total personality.

As we have already noted, the Catholic tradition is both Eastern and Western. To a large extent these cultural differences parallel the psychological differences between the *anima* and the *animus*, the female and male archetypes. Men say women are unpredictable, and Europeans say the Chinese are inscrutable. These are really two examples of the same phenomenon: the inability of one type of consciousness to understand the other. It is only when men develop their own feminine dimension that they can understand women (and vice versa), and it is only when Westerners allow themselves to be immersed in Eastern culture that they can understand why Orientals think and behave differently from Europeans.

Historically, Catholicism has had a Western *animus* and an Eastern *anima*. That is, exteriorly and organizationally the Catholic Church is masculine, but interiorly and spiritually the Church is feminine. To appreciate this we need to describe the differences between masculine and feminine consciousness, between the male and female archetypes.

First of all, masculine consciousness is analytic. Whenever it perceives reality, it wants to classify and distinguish the elements within it. Western philosophy began with Greek thinkers who wanted to penetrate the essential nature of reality in order to understand what makes matter different from spirit, what makes human beings different from animals and so on. Scholastic theology in the Middle Ages was renowned for the many distinctions it introduced into Christian thought, between substance and accidents, validity and liceity and so on. Modern science is a continuation of that same mode of thought, classifying everything from atoms to stars into different types and analyzing the data it derives from careful observation.

Feminine consciousness, on the other hand, is synthetic. When it perceives reality, it looks at the whole rather than at the parts. It prefers to take it all in and admire its beauty rather than to break it apart and figure out how it works. It is the soul of creativity, beginning with its intimate awareness of the growth of new life within the female body and extending to the creation of community and the beautifying of environment. It is the inspiration of art, poetically combining separate elements into new aesthetic combinations.

Second, masculine consciousness looks at things in terms of order and ranking. It sees a place for everything, and it wants everything in its proper place. It looks for clear lines of authority and responsibility in a chain of command. It likes organization and structure. Whether we look at military or political organizations, corporate or ecclesiastical structures, we see a reflection of the masculine archetype.

Feminine consciousness, on the other hand, looks at things in terms of wholes and relationships. The *anima* does not perceive linearly but connectively, radiating from itself at the center. Its model is not hierarchy but network; its ideal is not the structured organization but the family. The female soul (whether in a woman or a man) does not rank her children; she loves all of them equally. She sees the differences in each of them, but the differences do not make one more important than the other.

Third, masculine consciousness is fascinated by power and control. It loves to oppose things against each other and to set people against one another. Of course, it always wants to be on top, to be able to win whenever there is a conflict. Winning, whether in war or sports, in business or politics, in policy or doctrine, is all important.

Feminine consciousness, on the other hand, is more concerned with caring and bonding. Winning and losing are less important than being together and accepting one another. Indeed, there are no winners or losers, only those within the circle and those outside it. Right relationship is more important than righteousness; reconciliation is more important than conquest.

If we look at history, we see the feminine soul of Christianity most clearly in the Middle Ages. Although the external structures of the Church were masculine, the inner life of the Church was very feminine. The historian Henry Adams refers to that period of European life as the Age of the Virgin, in contrast to modern times which he calls the Age of the Dynamo. The dynamo is a machine for the production of electricity; its archetypal function is to get a single job done. The virgin is a woman who is open to the generation of life; her archetypal attitude is receptivity and patience.

Medieval spirituality, as we already have noted, was typified by devotion to Mary or, as it also has been called, the Cult of the Virgin. The Virgin was the spiritual archetype of the medieval Church, attending people's needs during the Dark Ages, assimilating the variety of ethnic cultures within herself, receiving new insights from her encounters with the Greek and Moslem cultures, patiently nurturing European life until its birth into modernity during the Renaissance.

Medieval Christianity was also feminine in its attitude toward the world. It honored prayer and contemplation in its monasteries and convents. It enjoyed play and festivity, declaring that on religious feasts peasants need not work and on holy days armies should not fight. It created the art of the cathedral and it promoted music and drama. It blossomed sacramentally into a liturgy of color and light, flowers and candles, incense and processions. It drew religion and culture together into the synthesis of medieval Christendom.

Although the lines of authority in the Middle Ages were masculine and patriarchal, the relationship of the Church toward its children was feminine and maternal. Except when heretics and critics challenged the authority of the hierarchy and were severely punished, the Church was tolerant and forgiving toward sinners. People could do almost anything and get away with it, provided that they confessed their sins and promised not to commit them again. And when they did commit them again, they could always go to confession again, and the Church through the priest would forgive them again. This is what we meant by saying above that the Catholic attitude toward morality is archetypally feminine.

Feminine morality does not live by rigid rules or conduct but by the fluid dynamics of relationship. Its ideal is the inclusiveness of the family rather than the exclusiveness of the clique or club. Above all, it desires unity, and it asks only that people observe the minimum standards of behavior to keep the community intact. When we look at the Church's reaction to divisive heretics on the one hand and to individual sinners on the other, we can see this clearly. The Church has tolerated all sorts of immorality and corruption, but when it has felt its unity threatened it has reacted with condemnation.

The shadow side of feminine morality is its unwillingness to make strong moral demands of people. It encourages people to be good and invites them to holiness, but it does not insist on the high morality of the gospel. Like a mother, the Church always wants her children to behave well, but if they do not she does not throw them out. Catholicism, for the most part, is very undemanding. In the selection from *Children of Sanchez*, Manuel shows us the dark side of maternal inclusiveness. People can live almost any way they want and still be Catholic.

No one can accuse Catholicism of being a narrow sect. It embraces saints and sinners, liberals and conservatives, personalists and pragmatists. Its tolerance of diversity, however, is also its weakness. Although it can easily form communities that gather together all types of people, it cannot form groups of radical disciples. It can tolerate such groups in the Church—and there have been many of them—but it does not form such groups itself, and it does not call the whole Church to a radical living of the gospel.

There is something very attractive about living the gospel radically, about accepting Christ's invitation to give up everything else and follow him. Certainly this is what Jesus demanded of those who listened to him, and this is how his first disciples responded to him. When we learn about the founders of religious orders or when we come across people who give themselves completely to the work of God's Kingdom, we instinctively admire them. We realize that this is what Christianity is really all about, and that there is

60

something passionately beautiful about this life-style. We know that we are missing something wonderful if we do not turn our life over to Christ, but as Catholics we do not hear the Church demanding that of us.

If the shadow side of Catholicism's masculinity is its authoritarianism, the shadow side of its femininity is its tolerance of mediocrity and sin. Even at the institutional level, the Church has winked at corruption, condoned war, lived with hypocrisy and complied with regimes diametrically opposed to Christ—often in the name of preserving peace and unity at all costs. When we count the cost in human suffering and unfaithfulness to the gospel, we can easily wonder whether it is too high a price to pay.

When we consider the alternative, however, we might think twice. No institution is perfect. Every community has its bright side and its dark side. If the spirit of Catholicism were not archetypally feminine, both its structures and its psychology would be totally masculine. It would be a completely patriarchal and rigidly demanding Church, and the starkness of its shadow would not be softened by the glow of femininity.

Consumer Catholicism

The feminine archetype, both virgin and mother, understands that the deepest joy comes through pain, that the greatest gain comes through loss. Through the pangs of childbirth she brings forth life, through the patience of giving she receives more than she surrenders, through the sadness of separation she offers her children their adulthood. The feminine spirit sadly yet gladly comprehends the paradox of death and rebirth. Feminine spirituality is taken up into the mystery of crucifixion and resurrection.

Catholicism has endured on the strength of its wholeness, holding femininity and masculinity within itself in fruitful tension. Were it not for its ability to bend and give, to embrace and gather around itself, to sacrifice for unity and forgive for reconciliation, it would have gone the way of sect

61

and empire, imposing itself briefly by force, then crumbling into history. Like the strong black grandmother of *A Raisin in the Sun*, the Church has been both receptive and assertive, both nurturing and powerful. The wisdom of its tradition has been to combine the zeal of the disciple with the patience of the teacher.

Today, however, Catholicism is in danger of losing its soul. The Second Vatican Council eliminated much of the medievalism in the Church but with it went much of the Catholic tradition's feminine spirituality. On the surface we can see changes such as the decrease in Marian devotion and the slow substitution of secular clothing for clerical dress. Beneath the surface, however, deeper and less visible changes are occurring.

The issue is one of spirituality. Spirit embraces many areas of life, certainly more than we can touch on here. For the sake of brevity, let us limit ourselves to the modern Church's intellectual life, its symbolic life and its prayer life.

Catholicism rightly prides itself on its intellectual tradition. The ancient Fathers of the Church—Athanasius, John Chrysostom, Augustine and a host of others—were mostly bishops who were the intellectual leaders of their day, writing theological and catechetical works, composing liturgies, debating doctrinal and moral issues in the public forum. The great universities of Europe—Oxford, Paris, Bologna and elsewhere—grew out of the monasteries and cathedral schools which preserved the wisdom of classical antiquity and gave it new life in a Christian setting. Through the Middle Ages and into modern times, the Catholic intellectual tradition preserved the liberal arts, the education which frees the mind for the art of living, as the basis for understanding the human world and the material universe in which we live.

A recent study of American universities concluded that of all the top graduate departments in the United States, not one is in a Catholic university, not even in the fields of philosophy and theology, which were traditionally Catholic strongholds. In the average Catholic college the requirement to graduate is no longer eight or 12 courses in philosophy and theology, as it was a generation ago, but two or four or six courses at the most. Catholic institutions of higher education are following the modern trend to substitute professional training for the liberal arts, the trend to put learning how to do a job ahead of learning how to live.

Many Catholic students today assume that that's the way it has always been, but in fact that is not so. The original idea of a university had little to do with career preparation and everything to do with preparation for life. Its objective was to impart the wisdom of the ages and to develop well-rounded persons. It was holistic rather than specialized, universal rather than narrowly practical. It was, we could rightly say, feminine rather than masculine.

The feminine ideal of education was to appreciate the whole picture before going on to specialized studies that analyze some portion of it. It was to comprehend the interrelatedness of things and to understand our place in relationship to them. It was to develop a sense of responsibility toward the world in which we live and care about the people who live in it. That feminine ideal, however, is now being lost not only among universities in general, but in Catholic universities as well. As more and more students major in technical and money-making fields, the great tradition of the pursuit of wisdom is being abandoned for the pursuit of self-interest.

The narrowing of our educational vision is paralleled by a shrinking of our symbolic vision. As we have already seen, Christians in the past were leaders in artistic creativity. In the ancient world the Church's sacraments developed from simple rituals to elaborately symbolic ceremonies that drew people into the experience of God and the contemplation of the Christian mysteries. In the medieval world Christian art and architecture, music and drama inspired people's imagination with a vision of realities unseen. In both our liturgical and artistic life today, however, there seems to be little creativity and little vision.

To some extent this lessening of Christian symbolic life is symptomatic of the world we live in. As our society becomes more pragmatic and technical, we have less incentive to contemplate and more incentive to manipulate. As our life becomes more busy, we have less time to appreciate God's revelation in the world around us. The result is that we are losing touch with the language of symbolism, we are losing our ability to be sacramental. Christians are not speaking to the world through their art; rather, it is the other way around. Most art in our society is commercial art.

Christian art, what little there is, is dully repetitious of past religious art. What gets produced is, quite candidly, what will sell. Liturgical music is limited to what can fit in missalettes, and few new hymns are being written. The liturgy itself is pared down in length and watered down in symbolism. New parish churches, often as not, are uninspired and uninspiring cinder-block rectangles. The Church, sadly, is not the patron of the arts it once was.

If anything, the Church should at least be the patron of prayer and the supporter of spiritual growth. We have every reason to wonder, however, whether that is really so. Besides the narrowing of our educational vision and the shrinking of our symbolic sensitivity, we seem to be suffering from a collapse of our prayer life as a Church.

Again, to some extent, this parallels what is going on generally in our culture. The visible symptoms are the increasing secularization of our society, the banning of anything remotely related to prayer and religion in public education and the separation of church and state with an intensity never intended by the framers of the U.S. Constitution. As Americans, we suffer from what is happening around us in our culture rather than, as in the past, influence what is happening in the culture.

In the ancient and medieval worlds, and until fairly recently in the modern world, becoming Catholic meant being introduced to the great Judeo-Christian tradition. In early centuries people were initiated into the Christian community through a lengthy process of personal conversion that culminated with 40 days of prayer and fasting in preparation for the Easter Vigil. In medieval centuries people were surrounded by a Christian culture that spoke constantly to them of the Jewish patriarchs and prophets, of Jesus and the apostles, of Mary and the saints. Today, as already noted, many Catholics grow up ignorant of their religious heritage.

Missing the facts about the past is not nearly as important as missing the values that the facts represent. There is a value in prayer that goes beyond asking God to grant our wishes. There is a value in meditation that is learned only in the experience of regular practice. There is a value in spiritual development that is represented in the stories of the saints and the writings of the mystics, but it is not discovered until one enters into dialogue with the heroes of the past and gradually realizes what made them great.

What made them great was the personal relationship with God they found in prayer and developed in daily meditation. They took time to listen to God calling them to a deeper level of reality than the world around them represented. They answered God's invitation to explore the spiritual reality at the center of their own being. They entered the narrow gate into the Kingdom instead of following the wide path to success and achievement in the world.

Although we hear a good deal about prayer in the Church today, we do not see people being really taught to pray. Catholic prayer life—apart from Sunday Mass, which is public rather than private prayer—has collapsed into talk about prayer, a step removed from the real thing. We learn to really pray, however, not by hearing about it, not by being told that we ought to pray, but by entering into the experience of prayer with others. Few opportunities to enter into that experience exist in the Church today.

Prayer is an archetypally feminine activity. It is not doing but being. It is not accomplishing but resting. It is not performance but relationship. It is a centering and focusing on God and a receptivity to the word that God speaks to us in silence. Prayer happens within and is expressed outwardly in symbol, whether those symbols be words or gestures or artistic creations. Perhaps the soul is going out of Christian art because prayer is going out of Christian life. Art expresses what is within, but if there is nothing within, there is nothing to express.

Paradoxically, our soul does not grow by being fed. It does not develop by taking more and more into itself, by adding experience onto experience, by increasing information or activity. Spiritual development is not a matter of addition but subtraction. It is not an aggressive activity but a passive activity, not a taking in but a letting go. It is not archetypally masculine but feminine.

Our American Catholic culture, however, like American culture in general, is becoming increasingly more masculine. It is becoming more accomplishment-oriented, more power-oriented, more consumer-oriented. We equate success with the ability to consume more and more. We idolize the life-styles of the rich and famous who have reached the level of conspicuous consumption.

This is why our universities have abandoned the search for wisdom, which is a feminine, inner activity, in favor of the quest for courses and degrees. We have become consumers of education instead of seekers of understanding. We do this not only in our schools. We attend lectures and workshops, we read books and articles, we listen to tapes and watch television, blindly believing that the more we take in, the better off we are. It does not matter whether what we are learning is secular or religious; the pattern and effect are still the same. We become warehouses of consumed and forgotten information because we do not take the time for our soul to sift through the trash and find whatever treasures might be hidden there.

Likewise, we have lost our sensitivity to art because of our assumption that more is better. Instead of being receptive to art, we have become consumers of art. Into every masterpiece the artist pours his or her own soul, which our own soul can connect with only by spending time with it in contemplation, developing a relationship with it. What we do, however, is race through galleries and museums to see as much as we can, without taking the time to see anything in depth. We collect consumer art in our homes, in the vain hope that by having more we will somehow be better off. Yet we do not even look at all we have.

Consumer religion has the same pattern, and the effect is

the same. We think that the more we go to church, the more religious we become. We think that if we get others to go to church that they will be spiritually better off. Yet by doing that we are not making them more Christian; we are simply making them more churchy. Neither we nor they are entering deeply into what Church and liturgy and prayer are all about. Our involvement with God remains superficial, but its shallowness is hidden by having so much religion in our lives. This type of religion can even be a form of addictive behavior.

Consumer Catholicism could very well be the end of the Catholic tradition. Were it to succeed, it would continue the pretense of Catholicism, but without its soul. It would perpetuate the masculine structures of the Church at the expense of losing the femininity of its openness to God. It would deceive us into thinking that as long as we have parishes, as long as we have schools, as long as we have educational and social programs, as long as we have religious goods and bookstores, then the Catholic tradition must be alive and well.

Consumer Catholicism, however, is the very opposite of what the Catholic tradition has been preserving for 2,000 years. It embodies all the worst in ethnic Catholicism, institutional Catholicism, unscriptural Catholicism and undemanding Catholicism, without incarnating the spirituality that they perpetuated. It is thoughtless, uncreative, unprayerful religiosity. It is activity without purpose, words without meaning, a shell without substance.

Chapter Three

How Can You Be Catholic in America Today?

In Chapters One and Two we talked in generalities and sometimes rather abstractly about the past, the brilliance of the Catholic tradition and the dark side of Catholic history. We spoke about Eastern and Western culture, about ethnic groups and nationalities, about masculine and feminine psychology. We saw how the good and bad in the Church's past cast light and shadow on the Church today. Now it is time to change the emphasis and be more specific and concrete, to talk about Catholicism the way it can be lived by individuals in particular communities. It is time to talk about being Catholic in the present and to look forward.

We asked at the beginning *why* be Catholic; now it is time to ask *how* to be Catholic. Like the first question, this one is also a new question. In the past people grew up knowing how to be Catholic. They learned their Catholicism by osmosis, as it were, drawing it from their family, their parish, their ethnic group. They did not ask how to be Catholic; they simply grew up being Catholic. Catholicism was in the air they breathed, in their mother's milk, in the food that nourished them. They knew how to be Catholic by the time they were old enough to realize that they *were* Catholic and that other people in the world were not.

If there is an advantage to growing up Catholic automatically, there is a greater advantage in choosing to be Catholic. Grace always works better in the realm of freedom and personal decision, something converts have always understood better than people born and raised in the Church. It is no mistake that some of the most articulate Catholics have been converts: St. Paul and St. Augustine in the ancient world; John Henry Newman and G.K. Chesterton not too long ago; Thomas Merton and Dorothy Day in our own times.

To choose to be Catholic is analogous to choosing to be Christian. Even Catholics have to make that choice. They have to hear God calling them to follow Christ, to surrender to God just as Christ did, to be filled with the Spirit just as Christ was. They first have to be willing to enter into a dialogue with God and then to respond to what they hear God saying to them. Once they say yes to that dialogue, they have to listen to where the Lord is leading them. They enter into a personal relationship with God.

Many beautiful people, many saints we might say in our Catholic way, enter into that dialogue but do not hear God calling them to be Catholic. Perhaps they see too painfully the dark side of Catholicism and none of its brightness. Perhaps they have never met a Catholic who has spoken to them of the Lord. Perhaps they have never even been in a Catholic church. On the other hand, there are those who hear God calling to them from within the Catholic Church, or to the Catholic Church. In the past they were mainly non-Catholics. Today they may even be baptized Catholics who hear God calling them to live their lives as Christians in the Catholic tradition.

Once people hear that call from God, their religious faith is no longer a matter of "have to's." They do not *have* to be Catholic; they do not *have* to go to Mass on Sunday; they do not *have* to believe in the authority of the pope. Rather, they *choose* to do these things because they are in a personal relationship with the Lord, and they hear the Lord asking them to follow him in the Catholic Church. This is a much more mature way of being Catholic than simply being born and raised Catholic. It is a way of being Catholic that is open to many more than it was in the past. It is a very contemporary way of being Catholic, and in our day when no one can force us to be Catholic, it is a very appropriate way.

What 'Being Catholic' Means

Before the Second Vatican Council, Catholics had a pretty clear idea of what it meant to be Catholic. Being Catholic meant going to Mass every Sunday and to confession at least once a year. It meant not eating meat on Fridays and fasting during Lent. It meant praying the rosary, making novenas and going to Benediction of the Blessed Sacrament. It also meant believing in the authority of the pope and bishops, in transubstantiation and the seven sacraments, in the Assumption and other doctrines that Protestants did not accept. Most Catholics tended to identify their faith with the external observances and doctrinal beliefs that set them apart from other Christians.

Since the Council, many of the externals in the Church have changed. Also, in the spirit of ecumenism, we place more emphasis on the beliefs we have in common with Protestants than on ones which separate us. As a consequence, many people have been hard-pressed to define what it means to be Catholic. In the 1970's and 1980's a fair number seem to have concluded that being Catholic just means being Christian but going to a Catholic church on Sundays. Others have come to the even more vague conclusion that being Catholic is pretty much the same as being good.

From what we saw in Chapter One, it should be clear that belonging to the Catholic tradition is not a matter of being just like all other Christians except for what church you belong to. And if we reflect on our own lives for a moment, it should become equally clear that being Catholic is not the same as being good.

To some degree, no doubt, we learn to be good Christians and good Catholics from the Church, but at the most basic level we learn to be good persons from our families and from others who are close to us, be they

71

Catholics or not. The goodness in our character comes not from any religious beliefs or practices but from being loved. Of course, we are good in the sense that we are created and loved by God, but we do not always see ourselves that way, and we do not always act that way. We learn to perceive ourselves as lovable, capable and worthwhile to the extent that we are loved and trusted, and are able to love and trust. What makes us good is not our Catholicism but our loves: those who love us and those who let us love them.

What, then, does Catholicism make us? What does being Catholic offer us? To return to a theme already seen, we can say that taking part in the Catholic tradition has the ability to make us wise. Catholicism offers us not knowledge so much as wisdom. Most people conceive of wisdom as something intellectual, something in the head. Catholic wisdom, however, is something very down-to-earth and something in the heart. To speak of it in another way, we could say that Catholicism offers us connectedness. Being Catholic means being connected.

The wisdom of connectedness is most powerfully symbolized in the Eucharist, the central sacrament of the Catholic faith. If we understand the Eucharist rightly, we understand that we are not alone. God is with us in the Eucharist, and we need only to open ourselves up to God's presence to experience it in the prayers and Scripture readings of the Mass, and especially in Communion.

Our connectedness in the Eucharist is therefore first with God. Being in relationship with the Lord, listening to the word and responding to the invitation to greater self-giving and greater holiness is a personal connectedness that comes from participating in the Eucharist.

There is another connectedness that is symbolized by the Eucharist, however, of which this individual connectedness is only the beginning. It is the connectedness of community. It is connectedness with others in the Body of the Lord.

The broader symbolism of the Eucharist is the Body of Christ, understood not just in Communion but through Communion. We do not receive the sacramental bread and wine alone. We receive it at a sacred meal with others. We all partake of one sacrament, one Body of Christ, and in doing so we signify that we are willing to be one Body of Christ. As St. Augustine said centuries ago, the Eucharist invites us all to become what we eat.

The connectedness of the Eucharist is also therefore our connectedness with one another. We are not alone. We are not isolated individuals. We are not in competition with each other but in communion with each other. This is what Catholicism in its best moments has so powerfully understood. This is also what, in our individualistic society, we often fail to understand.

Unlike other religions, Christianity is not just concerned with individual salvation. The gospel of Jesus is not that every individual can achieve nirvana quite apart from what is going on around him or her. The good news is not that individuals can attain some transcendental state of consciousness that others may fail to achieve. The gospel, at least as understood in the wisdom of the Catholic tradition, is that salvation is possible in and through the Church, in and through community. It is in our relationship with others, and in our relatedness with the world around us, that we experience the saving power of God.

Dorothy Day, the convert who all her life identified with the poor, understood this more than most of us. Of all the options open to her, she chose the Catholic Church because it is a church of the masses, a church that embraces the nobodies of society and tells them that together they are somebody. Together they are Jesus in the world; they are the Body of Christ. She was quite aware of the pretentiousness of prelates and the silliness of clerical games, but that did not prevent her from seeing that the wisdom of Catholicism is that Christ is present in the littlest of his brothers and sisters.

Christianity is not a head trip but a heart trip. It is not a matter of ideas but a matter of relationships. It is less concerned with growing in knowledge than with growing in love. It has less to do with thinking religious thoughts than with living like Jesus. The traditional Catholic devotion to the Sacred Heart of Jesus expresses this awareness in the Church.

By the same token, Christianity is not an escapist religion but an engaged religion. It is not a matter of running away from the world but of getting involved in it. Its key doctrine is the Incarnation, and its key symbol is the Crucifixion. Childbirth and crucifixion are both bloody affairs, and Christianity points to the birth and death of Jesus as the key moments in human history when God was immersed in our salvation down to our very flesh and blood. In Catholicism we emphasize the body of Christ as much as the spirit of Christ when we talk about the mystery of redemption. We say that to follow Jesus spiritual works are not enough. We also have to perform what used to be called corporal works of mercy, which today might better be called acts of social justice.

St. John puts it bluntly: "If you say you love God but hate your brother or sister, you are a liar" (1 John 4:20). The kind of "hate" that he is referring to is not necessarily active aggression. It can be passive neglect, uncaring and unloving apathy. In other words, if you say that you love Jesus but do not show it in your concern for other people, you may be into some kind of intellectual or escapist religion, but you are not really into Christianity.

Catholicism is one tradition which takes this very seriously. It sees that in the Old Testament God was concerned with people's well-being, freeing the Israelites from slavery in Egypt, giving the homeless a land in which to live, protecting the poor from the oppression of the rich. It sees that in the New Testament the early Christians gathered into communities and supported one another with food, clothing and shelter, besides sending money to the poor communities in other cities. It sees that God has always been involved in human affairs, and that Christians have always been concerned with one another's welfare.

Sometimes people accuse the Church of getting involved in politics, but that is one accusation that Catholicism is proud of. If you read about the Middle Ages, you realize that the Church was deeply connected with medieval politics— not politics in the bad sense of backroom deals and shady compromises (although that, too!), but politics in the original sense of involvement in public affairs.

The Catholic tradition is one of both inviting and testing religious commitment, of both validating and questioning religious experience. The Church says, "We believe that you love God; let us see you put that love into action. We accept that you have been baptized in the Spirit; let us see how you live in the Spirit. We understand that you like to pray; come join us when we pray together." Catholicism plays the devil's advocate with people's religious claims, stretching them beyond individualism and calling them into connectedness.

What 'Being Catholic in America' Means

If being Catholic means being wise in the sense of being connected, then being Catholic in America means being connected with what is going on in the United States right now. We saw in Chapter One that being Catholic implies that we have a universal vision rather than a limited vision. It implies that we be concerned with what is going on around us and not just with what is going on in our own individual lives. Catholicism is not "me and Jesus" Christianity but Christianity that is connected to community, and ultimately to a worldwide community.

At the same time, we must remember that individual Christians are also individuals, and that particular communities always exist in particular places. They have their individual problems and their particular concerns. No religion can be content to preach universal doctrines to the neglect of local issues. Any church that ignores people's real problems and concerns does so at its own peril. Catholics, even by reason of their church structure, should be able to think globally and act locally.

At this point, then, the universal vision of Catholicism must look inward as well as outward. Our vision must be microscopic as well as macroscopic. We have to focus on the way that people live their faith as individuals, as families and as parish communities in the United States today. We have to examine the network of connections that people are involved in and that enable them to grow in their connectedness with God and one another.

To be honest, most people are not concerned with the big theological issues that interest theologians and the clergy. Most people do not spend much time thinking about the revelation of the Scriptures, the doctrines of the faith, the administration of the sacraments or the authority structure within the Church. If they spend 5 percent of their Catholic lives thinking about such matters, that would be a lot. Most people put 95 percent of their religious effort into thinking about issues that touch their personal lives.

They want answers to such questions as: How can I live my life the way God wants me to? Is the way I'm living good enough, or is there a better way? How should I pass on my religious beliefs and values to my children? Why do I get so bored at Mass sometimes, and does that have anything to do with why my kids don't want to go to church? Are we missing something? Why does our society seem to be becoming less and less Christian? How can I deepen my own faith? Why doesn't our parish feel like a community? Where can I go when I need help in my relationship with God, with my wife or husband, with my teenagers? Where is the Church when I face unemployment, poverty or homelessness? Can the Church help me when I see crime in my neighborhood, drugs in my children's school, dishonesty in the company that I work for? How can I be a good Catholic, a good Christian or even just a good person in this complicated world I live in?

The strength of ethnic Catholicism is that it answered many of those real-life questions. It gave simple people simple answers to life's basic religious questions. It told people who they were and how they should behave as Catholics. It gave them a place to belong and a sense of their relationship to the world around them. Because it was religion that was lived out in daily life, ethnic Catholicism was able to provide people with an inner strength and an outer direction. In its own way it engendered a faith that was deep, strong and alive, not just in individuals but in entire parishes. As long as it lasted, it gave people an experience of being Catholic, not just an idea of being Catholic.

Ethnic Catholicism in America, however, is breaking down. The old parish is not what it used to be. Catholic families are not carrying on the customs and traditions of their grandparents. The cultural consciousness of Catholicism is dissipating in our pluralistic society. We think of ourselves as Americans first, as having a certain job or family role second and as Christians or Catholics third. We no longer are automatically, ethnically Catholic. As a result, we have little awareness of what the Catholic answers to our real life questions could be.

If we are to find those answers in the Catholic Church of today and tomorrow, we have to look at four areas of Catholic life which have become problematic in the vacuum left by the disappearance of cultural Catholicism in our country. For the sake of convenience, we can label these problem areas as religious experience, Catholic identity, Church authority and personal mission.

Religious Experience

Catholic religious life in the past revolved around the sacraments. The early Church adopted Baptism as a ritual of initiation into the Christian life, and it developed a ritual of reconciliation for those who had departed from that life and then wanted to return to it. The early celebration of the Lord's Supper evolved into an elaborate eucharistic liturgy of prayers, Scripture readings and communion for remembering and participating in the mystery of Christ. Christians entered into the service of the Lord in a married state through the Sacrament of Matrimony and into the service of God's people in the Church through the Sacrament of Holy Orders. When they needed healing, they received it through the Anointing of the Sick, and when they were dying, they received that same anointing in the form of Extreme Unction. The sacraments marked the key turning points in the Christian life from birth to death.

Besides the Church's official sacraments there were other

practices which came to be called sacramentals. Blessings with holy water and ashes, litanies to the saints and devotions to the Blessed Virgin, festivals and pilgrimages, relics and icons, the rosary and other forms of recited prayer—all these were ways that Christians in the Roman Empire and the Middle Ages learned about, celebrated and deepened their faith. As we noted in Chapters One and Two, Christians who lived in a world without widespread literacy used public ritual to carry on the Judeo-Christian tradition by interweaving it with their own cultural traditions.

In the ancient and religious world public symbols (usually in the form of ceremonies and rituals) were the chief means by which people entered into the experience of God. During the ages before the rise of individualism, collective consciousness and social practices structured most people's religious experiences. Their sacramental symbols told them that when they were washed and anointed their souls were cleansed and strengthened, so in those moments they experienced God washing away their sins and giving them the power of the Holy Spirit. Their liturgical symbols told them that Christ became truly present during the Mass, so at the words of consecration and at Communion time they experienced the real presence of Christ. They understood then when they told their sins to a priest and heard the words of absolution that their sins were forgiven, so in confession they experienced the love and forgiveness of God.

The rise of literacy and individualism in the modern world since the Renaissance slowly unglued the cohesiveness of collective consciousness, including collective religious consciousness. The Protestant Reformation was the initial manifestation of this splintering process, first dividing Christendom into two large camps and then subdividing Protestantism into a multitude of denominations. Now, four centuries after the Reformation, Catholicism too feels the tension of division between groups and the stress of disagreement between individuals. As modern individuals we tend to think our own thoughts and to guard our own feelings, even when we are together with others. We are not easily caught up into the traditional meaning of our collective symbols. Our sacraments no longer speak to us collectively as they once did, and as a result they do not easily move us together into experience of God.

Because the sacraments could speak objectively about the mystery of God, Catholicism in the past felt little need to talk about the subjective side of Christianity. Even our theology was overly objective in the way it analyzed and explained the history of salvation (as something that happened long ago), the mystery of God (as being "out there," up in heaven) and the process of redemption (as an objective fact rather than an experienced reality). The subjective side of our religion, our experienced relationship with God, was expected to take care of itself as long as people were collectively committed to the objective truth of Catholic teaching. Now that our collective consciousness is being replaced by a more individualistic consciousness, however, statements of objective truth no longer satisfy our subjective need to know God personally.

The Christians who are the most aware of this need are, of course, the evangelicals and pentecostals. Whether they are Protestant fundamentalists or Catholic charismatics, they insist on our need to experience God's love and to respond to it personally. They stress that knowledge *about* Jesus is not enough; we have to *know* Jesus and have an ongoing relationship with him in conversational prayer. They insist on the experience of being born again in the Spirit; they emphasize the importance of living by the power of the Holy Spirit. Some traditional Catholics get turned off by the clichés and enthusiasm of charismatics and evangelicals. This aversion should not blind us, however, to the fact that behind the strange language and behavior of those who claim they've come to know the Lord, there is a real and powerful religious experience which has energized their faith. Those of us who are not attracted by the externals of the pentecostal movement need to realize that there is a deep inner experience behind them. And those of us who cannot stand the fundamentalist preachers of television, radio and revival meetings need to be aware that many Catholics listen to them precisely because they speak about knowing Jesus as their personal Lord and Savior.

There is a need, therefore, to reawaken in the Catholic Church the religious experience of God which once was easily evoked by the sacraments but which now is not easily aroused by religious rituals alone. Without that experiential dimension to our faith, Sunday liturgies become dry, boring and dead. We celebrate the objective reality of the Eucharist, but there is no subjective foundation for our celebration. At the Mass the Father is present, but we do not experience his loving fatherhood; the Son is present, but we do not talk to him as brother and friend; the Holy Spirit is present, but we do not sense any vitality in our own spirit. We listen dully to the words; we repeat responses lifelessly.

This need has been recognized not only by the charismatic movement in the Church but by many other modern renewal movements. The Cursillo and the Focolare movements began in Europe and have spread around the world. The Christian Family Movement and Marriage Encounter began in the United States, and although they focus on marriage and family relationships, they often have the added effect of renewing people's relationship with God. Christ Renews His Parish and the RENEW program are attempts to revitalize the subjective dimension of Catholic life that many Americans have been drawn into in their own parishes. The Rite of Christian Initiation of Adults and Re-Membering Church have been implemented to awaken the experience of faith in new and former Catholics.

Besides these large-scale movements and programs, many good things are also happening in individual parishes, such as adult education programs, Bible studies, youth groups, retreats and days of recollection. There are even prayer groups and support groups which are not formally sponsored by any parish but which people join because they are attracted by the opportunity to open up to the subjective dimension of their faith. Nor should we forget the individuals who, for reasons of their own, embark on a solitary journey toward the Lord and through private reading, prayer and meditation discover the experience of God.

All these movements, all these programs, all these groups and individual searchings, however, have thus far reached only a fraction of American Catholics. Religious experience for most Catholics is still a problem area, still an unexplored territory. The majority are living in what is left of ethnic Catholicism, vaguely associated with the institutional Church, still attending the sacraments more or less, but without the experience of God which the sacraments are supposed to mediate.

Nonetheless, whenever spiritual renewal does begin, it always begins in the subjective dimension. Thus the first problem area is also the first solution area. We see now, at least, that to be Catholic in America today we must become personally and not just collectively Christian. Individually and in our parishes and in our Church as a whole we must become subjectively and not just objectively Catholic. We have to be open to the experience of God in our lives, and we have to find ways to invite others into that religious experience.

Catholic Identity

One strength of institutional Catholicism was (and still is, for many) its ability to give people a feeling of belonging, a sense of who they were. By identifying themselves with the institutional Church, Catholics were given a feeling of importance that they might not have had as individuals. As members of the Catholic Church, they belonged to a great tradition with a long history, one that displayed its greatness in its churches and cathedrals, its schools and hospitals, its liturgy and its hierarchy, especially the pope. Their identity with the Church also defined their relationship to God, to Jesus Christ and to non-Catholic Christians, for as members of the one true Church founded by Jesus Christ they could be certain that they worshiped God the way God wanted to be worshiped.

The trouble with obtaining a sense of who you are from an institution, however, is that such identity is impersonal. It

81

is not really a personal identity but an identification with something outside yourself. It is not a subjective identity, an awareness of who you are as a person with your own thoughts and feelings and relationships but an objective identification, a connection you have with some object that is not yourself. Such identity is therefore necessarily shallow. It does not reach your innermost heart, but it touches only the outer regions of your personality and behavior. The ease with which the first Protestants could reject their Catholic identity when they felt that the Church had become corrupted and the ease with which some Catholics today leave the Church to join other churches they find more attractive are two good examples of the shallowness of identifying with an institution.

The deeper and more genuine way that we discover who we are is through personal relationships. By learning that we are loved, accepted and respected by others we learn that we are persons who are lovable and admirable in many ways. By going out to others and loving them, caring for them, accepting them and respecting them, we learn that we are persons who have a capacity for love, understanding, growth and cooperation. Moreover, personal relationships are always particular. Those who awaken and call forth our personal capacities are always specific individuals with whom we have a special relationship. Our relatedness to the important persons in our lives, not our connections with church or country or place of work or other institutions, are what give us our personal identity.

We begin to discover our personal identity as Christians, therefore, when we develop a personal relationship with Jesus Christ. Whether we relate to Jesus as law-giver or advice-giver, rescuer or companion, friend or lover, is secondary. We relate to Jesus in different ways according to our own personality and our needs at different stages of our spiritual growth.

Any wholesome personal relationship is a light in our life. It brightens our world and illumines our sense of who we are in relation to everything else in our life. The best example of this is falling in love. When we fall in love, even the rainiest day is full of sunshine, even the darkest night is filled with light. In the same way, when we fall in love with Jesus our relationship with him brightens our life.

Let us picture that experience as a match being struck. A light goes on in our life that was not there before. Perhaps it happens because you have been searching for a deeper meaning in your life, a sense of purpose that has not been satisfied. Perhaps you have been wondering whether God is real, or you have been reading the Bible on your own, or you have been trying to discover whether prayer is more than the recitation of words. Or perhaps it happens, as was suggested in the previous section, that you are invited to some renewal program, and somewhere in the course of it the program succeeds in making you aware of your personal relationship with Christ. When we say yes to that relationship and enter into it, a match is struck. It is the first step in the renewal of the Church, even though it begins at a very individual level.

As we are well aware, a match burns for only a short time. If we want to dispel the darkness, we have to light another and another. Our relationship with Christ is often like that at the beginning. After the excitement of our first personal encounter with Jesus has faded out, we find ourselves wanting to rekindle it. No one can be thinking of God all the time, and so we tend to get involved in our day-to-day affairs, and we forget the Lord. When we notice that this has happened, we return to prayer in order to reestablish our experienced relationship with Jesus. In doing so we strike another match.

It often happens, if we are alone in our relationship with Christ, that we get tired of striking one match after another. Perhaps the busyness of our life squeezes out the time we had set aside for prayer. Perhaps, after a while, we begin to wonder whether the relationship we found is real, or whether we are just imagining it. We feel a need for some confirmation and support from others.

Likely as not, we seek out others who have had a similar experience of meeting the Lord. If our first powerful encounter happened during a renewal program, we might join a follow-up group such as those sponsored by Marriage

Encounter and Cursillo. We might join a prayer group in our parish or a Bible study in our neighborhood. We are looking for a place where we can check out our match with others who have had a similar experience and perhaps where we can discuss what we believe we have learned through our relationship with Christ.

Quite often, though, the group we join is focused on something other than prayer. True, we share a common experience in having come to know the Lord, but after we have established that (and frequently we just presume it) we tend to put it in the background and focus on something else. We might find ourselves in a book discussion group, or we might join some parish committee or organization just to be involved with some people like ourselves.

Regardless of its focus, the support group we have found is like a candle in our life. Even though our own match may flicker and fade when we are not meeting with the group, our involvement with the group sheds a steady light in our life. It gives us the reassurance we need that what we have found through our experience is real; it gives us an opportunity to rekindle that experience periodically; it gives us a steady light to guide us. Joining such a support group is the second step in the renewal of the Church at the local level.

Such groups do indeed renew the Church, for they draw people out of passive membership and into active participation in the life and ministry of the Church. Once such groups begin to form, however, they tend to remain maintenance groups rather than growth groups. That is to say, they maintain the initial commitment of their members without necessarily drawing them into a deeper involvement with the Lord. In addition, these groups maintain the programs and organizations of the parish and the diocese, but they do not lead to new ones. They remain at the level at which they were formed, giving some support to individuals and some support to the Church.

Many Catholics have taken this second step, but of course many more have not. Still fewer are the people who have taken the third step in their own spiritual renewal and the renewal of the Church. We might call it the move from support group to faith-sharing group or from maintenance group to growth group.

To offer another image in line with the image of the match and the candle already given, we can say that a faith-sharing group is like a flaming torch. It is a larger, more enduring lamp that gives off much more light and warmth. We can see its light not just when we are at group meetings or working on group tasks but also in our day-to-day life. We can feel its warmth not just when we are with the others in our group but also when we are away from them. For a faith-sharing group involves the development of personal relationships.

As its name suggests, the principal focus of a faith-sharing group is the relationship of faith: faith in one another and faith in the Lord. It is not a faith that is presumed (as is often the case in the support group) but a faith brought out into the open. It is not faith in the sense of beliefs and ideas but faith in the sense of trust and commitment. In a growth group faith itself becomes the focus of concern, and it is this concern with faith that leads to spiritual growth.

In such a group we are willing to talk openly about our relationship with Christ and our relationship with one another. Both types of relationship involve faith and commitment, but at the beginning our faith is always weak and our commitment is always partial. At the beginning we are willing to go only so far in trusting the Lord and trusting others, but beyond that we are hesitant. A faith-sharing group is a place where we can reveal the secrets of our hearts with our brothers and sisters, sharing the light that has been given to us and exposing the darkness that yet remains. The trust and honesty of faith-sharing overcome our initial hesitance and encourage us to grow.

Cardinal Newman a century ago observed, "So much holiness is lost to the Church because brothers and sisters refuse to share the secrets of their hearts with one another." A hundred years have gone by, and as a Church we have yet to learn the lesson of those words of wisdom. We have learned, to some extent, the importance of coming to experience the Lord and of becoming involved in support groups, but few of us have learned to step beyond that.

You might think that priests and nuns, at least, belong to faith-sharing groups, but all too often this is not the case. In rectories priests tend to talk about the business of the parish and the work that they are individually involved in. When they are through with that, they talk about what other men talk about—sports and politics and business, perhaps, and what is on television. They usually do not talk about what is really in their hearts about their relationship with God and their relationship with one another. Nuns in convents often are similarly distracted, although many sisters living in smaller households have begun to share more openly with one another. Women seem to have a greater facility at doing this than men, and the nuns who have formed faith-sharing groups are often holier (in the sense of being more whole, more fulfilled and happier) than their counterparts a generation ago.

Faith-sharing demands risk-taking, which is why many people resist it. Moving beyond talking about the externals in our life to being honest about what is going on inside us means exposing our weaknesses and shortcomings to others. We would rather not talk about dryness and the dead spots in our spiritual life, and we would rather avoid talking about the difficulties we are having in getting along with other people. By exposing so much of ourselves we make ourselves vulnerable to judgment and criticism from others. Yet there is no way to grow in prayer or to grow in trusting others unless we talk openly and honestly about the faith relationships in our life.

Dialogue at the level of faith-sharing is not, of course, all negative. We do not just share what is going wrong in our relationships with God and the people we are committed to. We also share what is going right in those relationships. We talk about the graces God has given us, the joys we have experienced through being in communion with God, the insights that have come to us in prayer. We talk similarly about the gifts that others in our group have given us; we affirm the good that they have done; we express our thanks for the care and attention we receive from them. The light that we share with one another, more than the darkness that

86

we risk exposing, is what makes faith-sharing such a torch-like experience.

If we have never been in a faith-sharing group, it might be hard to imagine that there is yet a further step that needs to be taken for the renewal of the Church at the local level. That further step should come as no surprise, however, to those who are familiar with the history of religious communities in the Catholic Church. The ideal of such communities, from the earliest monasteries founded by St. Benedict to the order recently founded by Mother Teresa, goes beyond faith-sharing to life-sharing.

People in religious communities make three traditional vows: poverty, chastity and obedience. Unfortunately, the purpose of these vows has become obscured over the centuries. Today we tend to think of them abstractly as the giving up of money, sex and freedom for the sake of earning a reward in heaven, but their original purpose was much more concrete and down-to-earth. Their fundamental purpose was to unite people in a shared life.

The vows pose three fundamental questions about the best way to live together: Do I make what I have available to others, or do I keep everything to myself? Do I love many others, or do I love a few exclusively? Do I do what others need me to do, or do I do just what I like to do? These are the fundamental economic, social and political questions which everybody faces sooner or later when they think about their relationship and responsibility to others. The traditional vows clearly state that the ideal life is a shared life.

Shared life is in many respects a free and willing communism. This ideal was present in the earliest Christian community, and it was emphasized again in religious communities whenever they were formed. If the Church had remained true to the ideal of shared life from the beginning, there would have been no need for separate monasteries and religious orders. If the Church had not relegated the ideal to the "religious" life but had insisted that it is essential to the Christian life, perhaps the world would have been spared the menace of totalitarian communism, which is actually a perversion of the Christian ideal.

In our own day not only monks and nuns but also laypeople are discovering the beauty and power of life-sharing. Every now and then we read about a group of people who have thrown their lives together and have taken the risk of living closely with one another. In our own country these groups are sometimes referred to as Christian communities, alternative communities or covenant communities. A number of them grew from seeds that were planted by the charismatic renewal, first into prayer groups, then into faith-sharing groups and finally into life-sharing groups.

The New Jerusalem Community in Cincinnati, Ohio, is one such group where people have been willing to risk taking this final step. The community grew out of a need of high school students in the early 1970's to continue the spiritual renewal that they had experienced on weekend retreats that Richard was giving. (Authors Richard Rohr and Joseph Martos were members of New Jerusalem Community when Richard first presented a series of talks on "Why be Catholic?" This book is based on those talks.)

The original support group grew from six to 12 to 24, doubling month after month until, by the mid-'70s, the weekly prayer meetings were being attended by well over 800 people. No longer comprised just of high school students, the prayer group included people from all over Cincinnati and from all walks of life. A core group formed the nucleus of this growing community. They planned the prayer meetings and headed the various ministries that were becoming needed, such as the Life in the Spirit seminar to introduce newcomers to the community, a tape and book ministry for spiritual enrichment, and a prayer ministry for spiritual healing.

In time, the faith-sharing of the core group led them to sense that the Lord was leading them to make an even deeper commitment to one another. After months of prayer and discernment, many of them decided to move to a single neighborhood called Winton Place, where Archbishop Joseph Bernardin had said they could use a small school and old convent no longer needed by St. Bernard's parish. The community renovated both buildings, and through literally hundreds of hours of meeting and praying and working together, New Jerusalem evolved into a life-sharing community.

As one of the community members once put it, "The difference between the average parish and New Jerusalem is the difference between a cruise ship and an ocean freighter. In the parish thousands of people are being served by a small group. In New Jerusalem we're all crew." Everyone in the community does something to serve the needs of others in the community, or to serve the needs of people in the neighborhood and the diocese where the community is located. The 300 or so adults and children in New Jerusalem join circles of perhaps five to 15 members—a group small enough to share faith and social life in a face-to-face and personal way. They support one another spiritually and emotionally and even financially, as best they can. They work and play and pray together, becoming a Christian family to one another. Most of the adults belong to one or more of the many ministries needed to maintain the life of the larger community—outreach, initiation, liturgy, music, pastoral counseling, religious education, building maintenance, ministry coordination and so on—or the ministries that New Jerusalem performs for people outside the community—parish renewal teams, peace and justice groups, programs for the neighborhood's elderly and youth, food and clothing distribution for poor people and so on.

The best image to describe such a life-sharing community is a blazing fire. Many persons contribute time and energy to the community, giving up part of their individual existence to maintain the fire. By being willing to give of themselves for the good of the whole, however, the light and life they generate is much more than they could ever produce separately. They receive more than they give to one another, and they have enough left over to share with others outside the community. They become, as Jesus said they would, a city on a hill, a light shining on a mountain, a beacon drawing others to themselves.

The communal identity of a life-sharing group such as

New Jerusalem is, of course, much greater and deeper than the institutional identity that most Catholics have with the Church. It is an identity that arises out of commitment, investment and vulnerability. To some extent these three qualities are found in support groups and faith-sharing groups, but as the images that we have used suggest, the other groups pale in comparison. When people are committed to one another at every level of life, their identity with the group is solid. When people invest their time and energy to the building up of the community, their identification with the groups is strong. When people get so close that they have to accept one another's weaknesses, their common vulnerability creates a deep bond between them.

Catholic Identity, Continued

The issue of community identity is so important that we need to explore what it implies for being Church at a local level. For most of us in America today, this means belonging to a parish. Since it is unrealistic to assume that the institutional Church is going to dismantle parishes and tell all Catholics to join smaller, life-sharing communities instead, we need to envision how such communities can be formed within and supported by the existing parish structures.

First and most fundamentally, we no longer can harbor the illusion that it is possible to be a Catholic in isolation. The message that our large impersonal parish structure broadcasts to our people is that it is all right to be an anonymous Catholic, not knowing or caring for other people in the parish. Despite pulpit rhetoric of "the parish family," most Catholics assume that it is enough to go to Mass once a week, and after that, to live their lives alone. The parish has taken on the characteristics of the modern microwave family, who come and go as they please, just stopping long enough in the kitchen to heat up some food for themselves. In the same way Catholics today seem to think they should just go to church to be spiritually refuelled and then go off for a week in their own individual directions.

The gospel of Jesus is not meant to be lived alone. The belief that the gospel can be lived in isolation comes from the individualistic tendency of modern culture. Christianity was not lived alone in the Middle Ages nor in the ancient culture that preceded it. From the beginning the gospel was meant to be lived by the Church, by a community of believers, by a Body of Christ whose members are connected with one another.

When people try to live the gospel by themselves, it becomes an individual philosophy rather than a communal way of life, a collection of abstract ideas rather than a revelation of how to live in holy and wholesome relationships. If there is anything that the New Testament teaches us, it is that salvation comes not by thinking in isolation but by loving and caring, forgiving and sharing with others. And since we develop a sense of our personal identity through our personal relationships, we come to know who we are as Christians primarily through our connectedness with others in a Christian community.

Attempting to live the gospel in isolation usually turns it into a set of beliefs that are not put into practice. Without the support of others, we are not willing to take the risks that following Jesus really demands. We are prone to play it safe, to do what is acceptable in the world around us. We fail to hear the gospel calling us and our society to radical conversion.

Unless we are connected to a Body of Christ that is united in its vision of the Kingdom, we feel naked and alone, afraid to change in order to enter the Kingdom and live out that vision. When we are confronted with hard questions such as the right to life, nuclear weapons and solidarity with the poor, we are not willing to admit that the gospel of Jesus has anything to say about them. The parish ought to be the place where Jesus can be heard addressing the crucial issues of modern society and where the hard questions can be confronted head on.

Second, then, we have to raise such questions in the parish, and we have to wrestle with them as a community.

We need to be asking what it means to be a Body of Christ living the gospel in our world today. By asking penetrating questions about our meaning and purpose as followers of Jesus, we come to a deeper awareness of who we are as members of his Church.

If we fail to ask such questions, we only placate those who are not truly interested in heeding Christ's call for conversion. If we do not raise such issues, we never challenge those who are ready to be challenged. Instead, we allow everyone to slip into the false complacency of being satisfied with the way things are in their own lives, the life of the Church and the condition of the world. Jesus' first words in his public ministry were a call to conversion and a challenge to enter the Kingdom: "The time has come! The Kingdom of God is at hand. Turn your lives around and believe the good news" (Mark 1:15).

Third, we have to acknowledge that the journey of faith is a process. Although everyone who has truly decided to follow Christ is willing to take some step in faith, not everyone is able to leap into life-sharing right away. In encouraging spiritual growth, therefore, the parish has to provide an environment for people to take the next step that is right for them, whether it is learning to pray, understanding the Scriptures, ministering to others, witnessing for peace or working for justice. There have to be many programs of evangelization and initiation into the Christian life, many different types of support groups, many opportunities for ministry, many levels of faith-sharing, many invitations to life-sharing. By entering into different group relationships at different stages of their faith journey, people can identify with those who have the same growing vision as they find their identity within the Church.

If we do not allow for such diversity in the Church, people can become quickly disenchanted and leave the Church after an initial burst of enthusiasm. They may make a Cursillo or go through the RENEW program, only to discover after a while that the program is no longer meeting their growth needs. Many prayer groups in the charismatic renewal experienced the phenomenon of people coming into the group, participating for a while and then dropping out. They may have been dissatisfied that the group was not leading them further, if it was not able to support them when they heard the Lord calling them to deeper conversion or to new ministries. Or they may have become uncomfortable with the direction of the group's leadership, but they had no options other than to stay in this one group or to try and go it alone.

By the same token, if there are not many support, service and growth groups in a parish, everyone will want to make the parish into something that meets their particular needs. The result is either the supermarket parish or the quick-mart parish. The supermarket parish spreads itself thin trying to do a little bit for everybody. The quick-mart parish gives up trying to supply so many different needs and concentrates on providing just the staples. In either case a small group of ministers is trying to do it all, and they are as involved in the lives of their people as the person at the checkout counter. There is no opportunity for deepening the personal relationships that build identity. Nor is there any vision of the Church other than the Church as a dispenser of spiritual goods in these types of parishes.

Fourth, besides being diverse, parishes also need to be directional. Individuals need a sense of direction if they are to grow, and small groups need direction and purpose if they are to have the cohesiveness required to keep them going. The same is true of the parish as a whole. Without a sense of direction in the large group, the parish stays on the map as a geographic entity, but it falls apart as a community.

There is a beauty in the circularity of the liturgical year, with its eternal recurrence of the mysteries of our faith. Like the regular routines of the family, the circular energy of ritual and repetition maintains a sense of familiarity and at-homeness which is needed for our identity as a Church. It is like the feminine energy of the mother who provides meals day after day and who prepares for birthdays and other family celebrations month after month.

Like the family, however, a larger community also needs masculine energy, which is directional energy. In the average American family the directional energy of the children comes from within themselves: They are growing toward maturity, developing their wings so that some day they can fly the nest. The directional energy of the parents comes from their personal goals: to make more money, to move into a larger house or a better neighborhood, to get an education or a more satisfying job and, we hope, to grow in their relationships and service to others.

To continue this analogy on a larger scale, the parish is something like a wagon train. The wagons have to be drawn into a circle every evening so that people can relax and get a sense of togetherness and have their needs attended to. The circular patterns in parish life provide the feminine energy for reinforcing relationships and caring for one another. At daybreak, however, the wagon master has to point the direction and take the lead if the people are going to get anywhere. Without the masculine energy that comes from having goals and purposes, people get locked into routines that go nowhere. Year after year they keep asking, "Do we need to go to Mass every Sunday?" "How far can we go before it is a mortal sin?" "Why can't we have a better CCD?" and other endlessly repeated questions.

The call of the gospel is completely absent from such circular concerns. The gospel, correctly understood, leads us beyond questions of housekeeping to questions of pathfinding. It leads us beyond being concerned with personal comfort and group preservation to becoming attracted by what is on the horizon. Walking together on the journey of faith keeps us moving toward the horizon, and being a people on the move heightens our sense of peoplehood.

Fifth, the parish's direction has to be both inward and outward. It has to be inward, toward seeking the Lord, toward making God the center of parish life, but it also has to be outward, toward the conversion of the world and the establishment of God's Kingdom.

This is why parishes need both prayer groups and task groups, both support groups and mission groups. Ideally, as any group within the parish moves toward faith-sharing and life-sharing, it will be both inwardly and outwardly directed, coming together for prayer and discernment, working together to accomplish some goal, coming together again for further reflection, then moving outward again on the journey of faith. An example of such integration is the Center for Action and Contemplation in Albuquerque, New Mexico, a spiritual training center that Richard Rohr established for laypeople in justice and peace work.

Unfortunately, many groups in the Church today tend to be one or the other type, rather than combining both. Either they focus on the feminine energy of building relationships or the masculine energy of accomplishing goals. When they do that, they often lose their identity as a community. Renewal programs and prayer groups that never move beyond the initial stage of discovering the Lord to discerning what the Lord wants them to accomplish as a group are likely to wither away. Task groups which do not take time to pray together, share faith together and support one another devolve into clusters of individuals trying to accomplish something on their own.

Too many religious orders, instead of being faith-sharing and life-sharing communities, have fallen into the trap of just being collections of individuals who happen to live in the same place. This is one reason why fewer and fewer young people are being attracted to the religious life. They see no need to belong to an order if they can perform a ministry without having to sign up for life. They feel no attraction to join an order if they do not see a community of people who are centered on the Lord and who can enter into the close and caring relationships that are needed for their personal growth.

At this point, you could reasonably ask whether there are any parishes where the five guidelines just enumerated are being put into practice—or is this model a whimsical pipe dream? Fortunately, it is not just a dream but a reality. Granted that it is a reality found in only a few places today, the fact that such parishes do exist proves that the Church can be renewed along these lines.

In every large city in America, and in some smaller ones,

there is at least one church such as we have been describing. Sometimes they are Catholic parishes and sometimes they are Protestant congregations, but they prove that the model works. Among the more notable successes are the Episcopal Church of the Redeemer in Houston, the College Hill Presbyterian Church in Cincinnati, Corpus Christi in Rochester, New York, St. Noel's in Cleveland and Holy Redeemer Church in San Francisco.

The New Jerusalem Community in Cincinnati, of course, is another example, although that is a Catholic community without parish boundaries. Other covenant communities, both Catholic and Protestant, have sprung up in a number of places around the country during the past 20 years. No two parishes and communities just mentioned implemented the model in exactly the same way. In fact, most of them grew up without such explicit guidelines. But looking back on the history of their renewal, each discovered and followed all five guidelines in some way or another.

The most outstanding examples of this renewal process, however, are to be found not in the United States but in the economically disadvantaged countries of the Third World. In Latin America, Africa and Asia the traditional parish structure is slowly being replaced by a new model, the "base community." In Brazil, for example, there are now between 80,000 and 100,000 such small communities which, for all practical purposes, are the parishes in that country. The large parish church has become the equivalent of a diocesan cathedral, and people go to it only on special occasions.

In a typical base community there may be as few as 10 or as many as 100 families located in an urban neighborhood or a rural village. In all cases the community is small enough that people know each other personally. They are aware of one another's practical and spiritual needs, and they pray together, study the Scriptures together and play together. They minister to each other, and they join together to address common problems. When a priest can come to the community, which is perhaps once a month, they celebrate Eucharist together. But when they do, they have something to celebrate: the spirit of the risen Lord living in a recognizable Body of Christ.

The renewal communities in our country and the base communities in the Third World are showing us that there is indeed a new way to be Catholic in the world today. If we look at what is happening to parishes in our own country, we could easily conclude that the Lord is slowly moving us in this direction. Although we pray for vocations to the priesthood so that we might perpetuate the traditional parish structure, God does not seem to be answering that prayer.

Perhaps the Spirit is saying to us that this is a new moment in history, a time when continuing in the old ways is no longer the best thing to do. The Holy Spirit poured the new wine of renewal into the Church at the Second Vatican Council, and now we are discovering that new wine needs new wineskins. Just as Jesus predicted, "No one pours new wine into dry wineskins, because the new wine will burst the seams and run out, and the skins will be ruined. New wine has to be poured into fresh wineskins!" (Luke 5:37-38).

It appears that our prayers for renewal are being answered, but in a far more astonishing manner than we ever expected. God seems to be telling us that it is time for the Church to find a new identity, for our old Catholic identity is being stripped away and we are being forced to find a new one. As the traditional Catholic prayer suggests, when God sends forth the Holy Spirit, the Spirit renews the whole face of the earth.

Church Authority

The third area of Catholic life which has become problematic is Church authority. In discussing the dark side of Catholicism we have already talked about the negative influence of authoritarianism and clericalism in the institutional Church. When we discussed the bright side of Catholicism, we also mentioned that authority is needed for the formation of community because, without some focal point of unity, individuals go their own way and communities fall apart.

What then is the authority which is needed for the renewal of the Church today? Where does the authority in the Church come from? There can be no doubt that the Church's authority ultimately comes from God. If the Church is the People of God and if the Church is God's instrument of salvation, then both the authority of the Church and any authority within the Church must ultimately derive from God.

Religion is necessarily authoritative. It is not something to be taken or left, picked up or discarded at will. It is not a matter of personal preference, like a hobby or a job, or a matter of individual opinion, like membership in a club or a political party. Religion makes ultimate claims about the meaning and purpose of life. No human authority can pretend to know what religion claims to reveal about the origin and destiny of human existence. If religion has any credibility at all, it is only because its authority comes from God.

God, however, does not reveal himself directly. As St. John says tersely, "No one has ever seen God" (1 John 4:12). God's revelation is always mediated, that is, revelation always comes to us through the medium of human experience. Whether God speaks in visions or voices, in feelings or hunches, revelation is being mediated through human imagination. Whether God speaks through Jesus or the Scriptures, through prophets or other religious authorities, revelation is always coming to us through the experience of seeing or hearing something besides the transcendent and invisible God.

In Catholicism we believe that God's revelation comes to us primarily through Scripture and tradition. The Scriptures embody the revelation that God gave to the Israelites through their history and the revelation that God gave to the apostles through their experience of Jesus Christ. The Catholic tradition embodies the wisdom of centuries of Christians who reflected on the Scriptures and sought to hear God speaking to them in their own lives. Although God can and certainly does speak to individuals, we believe that personal revelations always have to be judged according to whether they agree with the basic revelation of the Scriptures as understood in the Judeo-Christian tradition.

Not everyone, however, is a Scripture scholar or a student of Church history. For that reason Catholics also believe that the Church itself, and especially its pastoral leaders, have a special authority when it comes to interpreting the Scriptures in the light of the great tradition. The pope, bishops and local pastors are mediators of what God is revealing in the Church in the present day.

In Catholicism, therefore, we can say that there are various sources of religious authority. The ultimate authority is always God. The primary mediators of God's revelation are Scripture and tradition. The contemporary interpreter of that revelation is the Church, whose faith is expressed through its pastoral leadership. But we also believe that God speaks authoritatively to individuals, through their own conscience, for example.

One of the great benefits of being Catholic is that we are not alone when it comes to figuring out what it means to be Christian. Unlike Protestants in rather individualistic denominations, we are relieved of the burden of having to interpret the Scriptures all by ourselves or to decide between conflicting interpretations offered by countless writers and media evangelists. We are able to stand on the shoulders of those who have gone before us in the Catholic tradition, trusting that their experience of God was genuine and that their understanding of revelation was valid. We can turn not only to the basic statements of faith found in Church documents but also to the writings of those saints and theologians who have contemplated the Scriptures and who have wrestled with the same problems that confront us in our own lives. Our tradition gives us guidance for our own faith journey, at times reassuring us that others have heard what we believe that God is telling us, and at other times pointing out things that we have not yet noticed in the Bible.

At the same time, however, we must not forget that living the gospel is for each of us our own responsibility. At the heart of living the gospel is a personal relationship with God, and a genuinely personal relationship involves knowledge and commitment on our part. Once we have matured past childhood, we can no longer get along on inherited faith. If we are adult believers, we are not justified in saying that we believe because we have been told to. Nor is it credible for us to follow religious practices merely because we have been taught them. At some point in our religious development we need to take ownership of our beliefs and actions. Otherwise our faith is not truly ours but someone else's.

The purpose of being in touch with our religious heritage is not so that we can follow it blindly but so that we can learn from it intelligently. We should read the Scriptures not to be given easy answers to all our questions but to open ourselves up to God speaking to us through them. Likewise, we should acquaint ourselves with the Catholic tradition not to follow slavishly what has been done before but to search maturely for the wisdom of the ages. We cannot escape our responsibility by retreating into either biblical fundamentalism or doctrinal fundamentalism.

Being in touch with what the Church believes is another blessing that we as Catholics enjoy when it comes to understanding God's revelation. The Catholic tradition holds that besides the revelation that is to be found in the Bible and the Church's doctrines, the *sensus fidelium*, the "consensus of the faithful," is helpful for understanding what God is revealing to the Church at any given moment in history.

This continuous revelation in the Church is the basis of what Cardinal Newman called the "development of doctrine," the ever-growing comprehension of matters of faith and morals that have not yet been clearly spelled out in writing. During the first decades and centuries of Christianity, for example, the *sensus fidelium* decided which of the many early writings should be included in what today we call the New Testament. The doctrine of the Blessed Trinity, the establishment of the seven sacraments, the veneration that is given to Mary and the canonization of the saints all expressed the consensus of the faithful at various points in the Church's history.

If authority is a problem area in the Church today, it is partly because we have forgotten the importance of the *sensus fidelium*. Although ethnic Catholicism thrived on doing what seemed appropriate to people in a given culture (for instance, special festivals and unique religious customs), institutional Catholicism fostered the opposite habit of not doing anything unless the hierarchy approved of it. The problem was compounded by the fact that in many forms of ethnic Catholicism, authoritarian leadership was culturally acceptable. As we have seen in the previous chapter, paternalism in the clergy breeds passivity in the laity. But paternalism in the Church when society is becoming less patriarchal also generates resistance and resentment.

The problem today is not really authority in the Church but authoritarianism. The Church, like any institution, needs authority. Genuine authority inspires and leads: it authors a vision of creative possibilities and authorizes others to follow it into that vision. Authoritarianism, on the other hand, constricts vision and restricts the realm of possibilities; it tells others what to do and forbids them to do anything different.

When the hierarchy loses touch with the *sensus fidelium*, it tries to give orders, but, by and large, the people do not follow. The people have an intuitive charism for discerning what God is revealing to the Church in the present day, and if the hierarchy's interpretation goes against this, they are puzzled and dismayed by the lack of consensus. The temptation of authoritarian leadership is to insist ever more stridently that it speaks for God, but if the people do not hear God saying the same things to them, they withhold their consent.

This is not to deny that the hierarchy must also take the lead in teaching what has not yet become generally accepted by the laity. The American bishops were criticized for the stands they took against nuclear war and the policy of deterrence, and the pope himself was criticized for speaking out against the injustice caused by unrestrained capitalism. The hierarchy is entrusted by God not only to follow but also to form the *sensus fidelium* in matters of faith and morals.

If we glance at some of the tensions between the

hierarchy and the laity in the Church today, however, we can observe that often the real issue is not authority but authoritarianism. There are many differences of opinion that involve sexuality because patriarchal leadership is not comfortable with nontraditional sex roles and practices. The ability of women to serve in church ministries, the place of women in the family and society, and the morality of certain sexual practices are some of the more debated areas between the celibate male hierarchy of the Church and the married and unmarried laity who constitute 99 percent of the Church's membership. Too often the hierarchy appears to have made up its mind without sufficiently listening to the people whom its decisions affect.

Sexuality, however, is not the only area of disagreement. The ability of theologians to articulate the *sensus fidelium* in words that do not conform to the writings of the past is sometimes not recognized by conservative Church leaders who forget the development of doctrine. In a changing world the way we talk about the gospel has to change if our religious language is not to become archaic. For doctrine to develop there must always be some who are at the cutting edge of this process. The people in the Church either come to recognize their Catholic faith in the writings of these thinkers, or else they do not. If they do not, the writings gather dust and are forgotten. But if the faithful do recognize an authentic expression of the Catholic faith in them, the writings of these theologians become more authoritative in the Church. The final stage in the process arrives when the hierarchy recognizes the consent of the faithful and officially approves what the Church has accepted.

When the hierarchy does not recognize this process, conflict occurs. It has occurred in the past, and it is occurring in the present. Even the greatest theologian of the Middle Ages, St. Thomas Aquinas, was condemned more than once by his local bishop, yet a few centuries later his writings became the standard textbooks in theology. A few decades ago Pierre Teilhard de Chardin was silenced by the Vatican for his views on evolution, but after his death his views helped many Catholics to see evolution as the work of God.

In our own day, Hans Küng, Leonardo Boff, Charles Curran and Matthew Fox have been singled out for expressing unorthodox opinions, and the authoritarian manner in which they have been treated has caused conflict in the Church.

Another area of disagreement is the right of people to form eucharistic communities which are not headed by priests. This conflict is not as visible in our own country as it is in countries where there is a great shortage of priests, but it is approaching our own shores as the priest shortage becomes more acute. Laypeople in the base communities mentioned earlier, for example, would like to celebrate the Eucharist more than once a month, but they are prevented from doing so by Church laws that forbid the ordination of married men. The proponents of liberation theology in the Third World argue that the people should be freed from such ecclesiastical restrictions, but the hierarchy is not yet open to change.

The hierarchy has to be conservative, for one of its duties is to conserve the Catholic tradition. A hierarchy that was so unmindful of the past that it permitted anything and everything to pass itself off as Catholic would not be fulfilling the office entrusted to it. At the same time, however, a hierarchy that was so mindful of the past that it could not allow development and change would equally betray its trust. Today our bishops are better able to distinguish between mere modernistic updating and more radical returns to the original gospel (for example, nonviolence and pacificism, community, simple life-styles, lay ministry). Both concepts look like change but have very different sources, energy and goals.

Catholics ought to appreciate change more than anyone else. Ask Catholics what happens at the Eucharist and they say that bread and wine are changed into the Body and Blood of Christ. Change is at the heart of the basic symbol of our faith, the central sacrament of our Church. Change is at the core of our theology, not only in the theory of transubstantiation but also in our whole theology of the sacraments and in our whole spirituality. Through the sacraments God gives us new life, and through spiritual growth our life is constantly renewed. As we shall see in Chapter Four, the greatest examples of change in the Church are the saints, for through their openness to the Spirit they let God change them radically and continuously.

The example of the saints also gives us the basic answer to the problem of authority in the Church. Saints are ordinary people who become extraordinarily holy by being obedient to the authority of God. They listen to God in their own hearts calling them to radical conversion and continuous reconversion. They read the Scriptures with an openness to the word of God, and they are mindful of the Catholic tradition of interpreting that word. They have a sense of what God is revealing to the Church in their own day, and they respect the pastoral leadership in the Church.

As a result of their obedience to the authority of God as it is mediated through their own prayer experience, through Scripture and tradition and through the Church and its leaders, the lives of the saints take on a unique authenticity. It is the authenticity of the gospel shining through them. Because of the gospel authenticity of their lives, the very way they live bespeaks the authority of God. People are attracted by that authenticity and they respect the authority behind it. It is no coincidence that most of the founders of religious orders and spiritual movements in the Church have been saints.

What can be said of individual saints can also be said of authentic Christian communities. When people are authentically living the gospel in a Body of Christ, their communal life speaks with the authority of God. When people are sharing and caring for one another, when they are loving and forgiving one another, when they are living in God's Kingdom and working to bring God's peace and justice to the world, their community develops an authority that others want to listen to and learn from.

Credible authority in the Church, from the time of the earliest community to the present, comes from the authentic living of the gospel. It is an authority that is not authoritarian but authoritative, not demanding but inviting, not bad news but good news. The authentic living of the gospel is not a dead authority but a living authority, calling people to convert from death to life, showing them Jesus' way to live life to the fullest.

In the Church today we need to rediscover this vital meaning of religious authority. If we not only preach the gospel but live it, our lives will have gospel authenticity and our preaching will be received as authoritative. If parents authentically live the gospel, their children will see it for the good news that it is. If the gospel is lived in communities and parishes, they will have the authority of Jesus in the neighborhoods and cities that surround them. And if the gospel is lived by the Church around the world, the Church will have all the authority it needs to be God's instrument of salvation.

Personal Mission

Our discussion of authority has naturally led us to the fourth problem area in the Church today—that of mission. The fundamental mission of the Church is to live the gospel and, by doing so, to announce the good news of salvation to the world. If the Church is the people of God, however, its mission is the task of the whole people, not just of a designated few. If the Church is to live the gospel, then everyone in the Church must live the gospel. It is the personal responsibility of every member of the Church. If they fail in this responsibility, then the Church fails in its fundamental mission.

Institutional Catholicism, under the influence of Western culture, developed a very organizational approach to mission. During the earliest centuries of Christianity, most of the missionary activity in the Church was performed by ordinary Christians living their lives in such an extraordinary way that others were attracted to their way of life. Except for a few unique individuals like St. Paul who traveled from city to city to announce the good news about Jesus, we have no records of any organized missionary efforts in the early

105

Church. The good news was spread by people simply living the gospel, and the authenticity of their lives was all the authority they needed that the gospel was the means to salvation.

The first organized missionary efforts took place a few centuries later, after the collapse of the Roman Empire. The Eastern world was virtually cut off from the West, and the bishop of Rome took it upon himself to ask monks to leave their monasteries and risk their lives to bring the gospel to the barbarians in northern Europe. Many men died heroically in the effort, but in the end their courage prevailed. By the ninth century the majority of Europe was converted to Christianity, and by the 11th century the job was done. That vast and prolonged missionary effort gave rise to medieval Christendom.

Those centuries of missionary activity, however, set a pattern for all missionary work in the future. No longer would individual Christians see their mission as living the gospel with such authenticity that others would be attracted to it. For one thing, the whole of Europe was at least nominally converted to the Christian faith and there was no one left to baptize except infants. But the more important thing was that Catholics forever connected missionary work with those in religious orders. An important part of the early Catholic tradition was forgotten.

Ethnic Catholicism continued the pattern established during that missionary period. Unlike St. Paul, who preached the gospel and then left local converts to lead and build the Christian communities he founded, the monks established themselves as the leaders in the Church, and instead of building communities, they built monasteries. Those inside the monasteries were expected to live the gospel to the fullest, but those outside were asked only to obey the minimums of a moral life. A two-tier system of holiness was set up, with clergy on the upper level and laity on the lower level. The laity were dependent on the clergy for direction and correction. Their responsibility was only to "save their souls" by obeying the Ten Commandments and Church laws. Any responsibility for mission was left up to the clergy.

This is not to belittle the heroism of the missionaries in the Church during the past 10 centuries or so. Many members of religious orders, both men and women, spent their lives living the gospel and bringing it to people who would never have known Christ were it not for their dedication to the mission of the Church. That Christianity today is not just a European religion but a universal Church is due to the efforts of missionaries in the 16th century onward who brought the gospel to North and South America, Africa and Asia and the Pacific.

Geographically, their efforts succeeded. Evangelistically, however, their method failed. That is, the method that was institutionalized by the Church to bring the gospel to the world succeeded in bringing only the institutional Church around the world. The gospel was never lived fully by the whole Church, even in "converted" Europe. At best, the missionaries succeeded in civilizing the barbarians. The wars that plagued the European continent from the Middle Ages to the 20th century testify to the failure of institutionalized missionary efforts to truly evangelize. Nor should it be any surprise that in our own day one of our greatest needs is evangelization—within the Church!

Evangelization means, quite simply, living the gospel in such a way that others are attracted by it and invited into the Church. It is different from evangelizing, which means preaching the gospel and baptizing people into the Church. We are very familiar with the whole evangelical scene in the United States today, thanks to the notoriety of television preachers. Evangelism in our country has become a religious version of musical chairs in which people get converted into one church or TV ministry for a while, only to get disenchanted after a while and hop into another church. The preachers are simply reconverting the converted, rebaptizing the baptized. Their audience are the people who are into religion and enjoy doing churchy things like attending services and talking about theology.

The world does not need this narcissistic substitute for Christianity. It does not need this shallow spirituality of people endlessly wanting to be assured that God loves them, that Jesus died for them and that they are going to heaven. What the world has always needed, and what the Church needs today, is not just the preaching of the gospel but the living of the gospel.

The evangelization of the institutional Church, though, can never happen if it is left to the clergy, or even to a specially trained group of lay ministers. If evangelization means learning to live the gospel, we cannot pay others to do it for us. We have to do it ourselves. Otherwise we fail in our fundamental mission as followers of Christ, and the Church fails in its fundamental mission to live the gospel.

Living the gospel does not mean memorizing Bible passages or attending prayer meetings any more than it means memorizing the catechism and going to Mass. It does not mean having the answers and going to church but living the answer and being the Church. It does not mean simply obeying the Commandments, which is Old Testament morality, but enjoying the Beatitudes, which is New Testament life-style.

In many translations the Beatitudes, which are found in Jesus' Sermon on the Mount, begin with the words, "Blessed are..." (Matthew 5:1-12). Another translation of the Greek word that each beatitude begins with, however, is "happy." In this sermon Jesus is announcing his way of happiness, his way of living in the Kingdom. He says that happiness is found in being deliberately poor, in mourning with those who sorrow, in being down-to-earth, in doing what God asks, in being merciful and forgiving, in being single-minded, in working for peace and justice. The gospel is called good news because it is a way of living that leads to happiness, not only for those who live it now but also for those others who benefit from it.

Jesus did not simply preach the gospel, however, he lived it. The good news was first the life of Christ before it was ever talked about and preached to others. The good news was that it was possible to live the way that Jesus lived, and Jesus was the living proof of that new life. It was the life that was given to him by God, the life that could make all people sons and daughters of God.

In a word, the life of Jesus was a life of ministry. It was a life of service and self-giving. It was a life of laying his life down so that others might live. It was a life of crucifixion, and in Jesus' case crucifixion ultimately was a physical reality. But it did not end there, for it led to resurrection. In our case crucifixion may not be physical death, but it still means laying down our life that others may live. And it still leads to resurrection. That is the good news.

The life of Jesus, as those who have tried it know, is a happy life. There is no life that is happier or more blessed. It is a life of suffering, but it works miracles. It is frustrating, but it is rewarding. It means dying to self, but it also means being born again. It means making enemies, for it entails working for peace and justice, but it is a way to deep and lasting friendship, for it involves faith-sharing and life-sharing.

The life of Jesus is rooted in serving, healing and advocacy for others. For us today it is a life involved in the issues of homelessness, the care of AIDS patients, refugees, militarism and nuclear disarmament, prisoners and prison reform, welfare reform, battered and abused shelters, hospices for the sick and dying, poverty and many others.

It is not easy, perhaps it is not even possible, to live the life of Jesus alone. This is why for those who follow Jesus it is necessary to be a church, a Body of Christ. The mission of each Christian is to live the good news, just as Jesus did. But the mission cannot be accomplished, realistically, without the support of sisters and brothers in the Lord. When the Church lives the gospel, then individuals can live it. And when individuals live the gospel with one another, the Church's mission is fulfilled.

If the Church is to be renewed in our day, therefore, it must be through the new life that Jesus has given us and made possible for us. It must be through living the gospel and being good news. But that can only happen if each of us makes Christ's mission our own personal mission. That can only happen if we make our mission in life to be saints and to help one another be saints.

Chapter Four

Who Are Our Heroes and Heroines?

In this last chapter we shall return to the question we began with, namely, Why be Catholic? When we asked that question in Chapter One, we answered it by explaining some positive aspects of Catholicism. As we turn again to that question, we shall try to answer it not by talking about generalities but by talking about individuals. We shall be talking not so much about Catholicism as about Catholics.

When most people inquire about religion, they are less interested in abstract ideas than they are in people. They are not convinced of the truth of Christianity unless they can see it being lived by real Christians. If they meet someone who is a living example of Christian faith, they can imagine how they too might live if they had such faith. If they meet a follower of Jesus who is living the gospel, they can overcome whatever intellectual problems they might have with Christianity. If they meet a group of Catholics who exemplify Catholicism for them, they can deal with the shortcomings and failures that they see in the Church.

The same can be said of us, if we are trying to understand our own Church and wondering, perhaps, why remain Catholic? One of the best ways to understand our own religious tradition is to recall that litany of individuals whom we recognize as having been great Christians. For in the end, Catholicism is not so much a history of ideas as a story of a people, and the people we call saints are the heroes and heroines of that story. They are at once the paragons of Christianity and the paradigms of Christian living.

If we read the history of Catholicism, we come across many times when the Church was beset with problems. Sometimes they were problems that came from without, such as persecutions and invasions. More often than not they were problems within, problems of malaise and ineptitude, of conflict and unforgiveness, of moral and political corruption. For a while the Church would remain deadlocked and unable to resolve the crisis, but eventually something would happen that would overcome the problem. Usually that something was a someone, some individual who could show the way to write the next new chapter in the Church's story. And such individuals were quite often saints.

Some of the greatest saints were able to envision new ways to live the gospel when the old ways had lost their power. Some were practical people who did not write much but who had a gift for trying out new things. Some were thoughtful people who perhaps did not do much except write. In rare cases some were both pragmatic and intellectual, but all of them were prayerful, and all of them lived the gospel in ways that fit their time and place in history. Their living of the gospel is what made their actions and suggestions credible. The authenticity of their lives enabled others to trust them and to follow what they said.

By and large, Catholics have followed the example of their saints more than they have the ideas in their doctrines. Ideas are abstract, but lives are real. Doctrines can be hard to understand, but actions are easy to see. People are often bored by theology, but they are always fascinated by saints. Saints fire our imagination; they stir up our hearts; they awaken our dreams. They give us new ways to image reality and new ways to envision the future. They open up new possibilities for living the gospel, for they show us how they have already done it.

Theologian Richard P. McBrien, in his book *Catholicism*, helps us to understand why this is so:

Catholicism has never hesitated to affirm the "mysterious" dimension of all reality: the cosmos, nature, history, events, persons, objects, rituals, words. Everything is, in principle, capable of embodying and communicating the divine.

The Catholic tradition is one of encountering the invisible God in and through the visible world. Catholics are attuned to seeing God in people's lives and in what is going on around them, more than they are disposed to finding God in theological doctrines. To some extent, this explains the Catholic fascination with saints and the difference between the Catholic and Protestant traditions. Protestantism, with its emphasis on the preached and written word, has often had difficulty with the Catholic insistence on the visible, material and personal mediation of God. Catholicism, on the other hand, has always been comfortable with sacrament and ritual, with the Blessed Mother and the saints.

The Catholic vision that McBrien speaks of is not just theoretical. Catholicism has always found the divine within the human. God's love is incarnated in the unconditional love that people have for one another, and God's forgiveness is mediated by people unconditionally forgiving one another. The reason for the Sacrament of Reconciliation, for example, is not so that we can be told that God above forgives us here below. We reveal our darkness to another human being so that we can honestly experience the self-revelation that is needed for complete openness to God, and so that we can experience God's love and forgiveness coming to us through another human being. Believing that we are reconciled is one thing; experiencing it is quite another, and much more important for our spiritual growth.

Ultimately, the spiritual and the material worlds are one, for they are both God's world. For us humans, who are both matter and spirit, the spiritual realities of love, forgiveness, honesty, justice, knowledge and so on are always mediated by material realities that we can see, touch, feel and hear. If we were pure spirits, we could be purely spiritual with God. As it is, we always encounter God in and through our bodies. Even when we meet God in our private prayer experience, our very material brain is always working to make that experience possible.

For Catholics, then, God's grace is always mediated through human experience of one sort or another. The grace of Jesus Christ was revealed to the apostles through their experience of him. The grace of the sacraments is mediated by the experience of the people who participate in them. In the same way the saints have always been mediation points of grace, for they make the reality of God historical and visible, tangible and credible.

The saints of every age have revealed the truth of Jesus to that age. We can see how God was revealing himself at any point in history by looking at the saints of that period. Because of their openness to God they were mediators of grace and they radiated that grace to the world around them. In the lives of the saints we can discern how God works in human life.

We need reference points like the saints because, without them, we are all too likely to make ourselves the standards when it comes to living the gospel. We can read the New Testament, but we always look at it through our own eyes. We can study the Church's teachings, but we always filter them through our own biases. Unless we ourselves are saints, we are not likely to arrive at an unbiased understanding of the gospel.

Although each of the saints had their own particular way of viewing and living the gospel, all of them were unbiased in the sense that they put their selfish concerns aside and opened themselves radically to the truth that God was speaking to them. They were in as total a union with God as it is humanly possible to be. They threw themselves completely into doing not what they wanted but what God wanted. They surrendered themselves wholly, which is what made them holy.

In the pursuit of holiness the main obstacle is the self. It is not the circumstances that we live in, the people around us, or even the devil. The self is selfish, self-centered and self-protective. It does not want to surrender, to give up, to give in. The self that we have become stands in the way of self-transformation. The self that we believe ourselves to be does not want to be converted.

The saints are the heroes and heroines of the Christian life because they took the most courageous step of moving beyond the self to encounter the divine. They put the self aside to stand naked before the Lord. They emptied out the self in order to be filled with God. Having gotten rid of the self, they were receptive to the wholly Other. Having taken the wholly Other into themselves, they allowed it to transform their lives and make them holy.

In that one respect all saints are alike. In other ways, however, they are as varied as the periods in which they lived, the circumstances in which they found themselves and the personalities they had. For both reasons it is difficult to categorize the saints, since they are all alike and yet so different. Nevertheless, the Church in its liturgical calendar classifies the saints in various ways into martyrs, confessors, virgins and so on. We shall follow some of those classifications here, but we shall also use some categories of our own to show how they were all differently the same in heroic holiness.

Martyrs

The earliest heroes and heroines in the Church were its martyrs. Because they were all put to death, we tend to identify the word *martyr* with dying. The Greek word *martyrein*, however, means simply to give witness or testimony. Martyrs are Christians who give the ultimate testimony to the truth of the gospel. The good news is that God's life is so real and vital that not even the threat of death can diminish it and not even death itself can put an end to it.

We read about the first martyr, Stephen, in the Acts of the Apostles. He probably never imagined that he would ever be called a saint. He just wanted to bear witness to the truth of Jesus in his life, but those who did not want to hear that truth stoned him to death. In his life he gave everything to Christ, and rather than take any of it back, he gave it all away. His death, his martyrdom, was simply a continuation of the way he lived.

St. Stephen was killed because he had committed a religious offense—proclaiming Jesus as the messiah. If we look at many of the martyrs through the centuries, however, we cannot say that they were always killed for religious motives. In early Rome being Christian was a political offense, as was being Catholic in England during the Reformation. The Japanese martyrs in the 17th century were killed for reasons that were more cultural and nationalistic than religious.

Whatever the system they witness against, though, saints are always a threat to the system. Their inner freedom does not fit into any rigid system. Their spiritual strength enables them to defy any oppressive system. They can and do refuse to bow before idols, whether those idols be gold or silver, dictators or juntas, guns or tanks. Sometimes we forget this when we hear of Christians being killed in Latin America or South Africa. We are tempted to attribute their deaths to political motives, as if that discredits them as martyrs.

The martyrs of the first century all died for political reasons since they defied the coercion of the Roman Empire. Lawrence, Lucy, Agnes, Cecilia and many others died because they were caught belonging to an illegal movement. Rather than surrender their allegiance to Christ and betray their community, they carried their testimony to the limit and allowed themselves to be put to death. They became the heroes and heroines of the community, the first saints in the early Church.

Their names were remembered in the prayers of the Eucharist, and when their bones were buried in the catacombs of Rome the community celebrated their victory by sharing the Eucharist on their tombs. It was as though even their bones radiated the same spiritual energy that they themselves had radiated in life, and Christians wanted to be near them to be energized by the spirit of the martyrs. This desire developed into the practice of laying bones of the martyrs in the altars of churches that were later built in their memory, and for centuries Catholic altars always contained at least a few relics of the saints.

There is a saying that the blood of martyrs is the seed of the Church, for whenever there are such witnesses to the gospel the Church grows. As a matter of historical record, the number of Christians grew enormously during the period of Roman persecution. People wondered what motivated such heroism, so they sought out the Christian community and were evangelized. Perhaps the Church is not growing today because there are fewer martyrs. Since we no longer have to die for Christ, people sometimes wonder what we live for.

Nonetheless, wherever heroic Christians confront oppressive systems there are martyrs, and their lives radiate the same energy that shone out from the catacombs. They transmit life and energy and hope to those who see their witness and, later, hear about it.

In 1943 an Austrian peasant named Franz Jägerstätter stood against the Nazi regime that told him he must join the army and fight for the Fatherland. He stood very alone, for even the institutional Church was telling him that he ought to obey the government. He chose instead to obey what God was telling him, and he chose to be killed rather than kill others. Some may say that he used poor judgment, that he ought to have listened to the Church, that he was not really a martyr but a political casualty of war. Yet decades later we have forgotten the names of all the others in the story, while his still shouts freedom and encouragement to others.

Even more recently, as if redeeming the hierarchy from its support of military regimes, Archbishop Oscar Romero was murdered in El Salvador in 1980. He stood against government terrorism in his country, and he proclaimed the freedom of the gospel to his people. When he was shot by a death squad while celebrating Mass in a hospital chapel, some again said that he died for political rather than religious reasons. Yet today he is honored as a martyr by the poor of El Salvador.

People can try to judge dispassionately whether Christians who are killed for their beliefs are really martyrs or not, but in the end martyrdom is not judged dispassionately. The martyr's witness is a passionate commitment to the gospel which can only be judged by the spiritual energy it radiates, even from beyond death. Jesus said "by their fruits you shall know them" (Matthew 7:16). The fruit of martyrdom is life and hope and wholeness transmitted to others. Wherever such fruits are found, their seed is blood that has been shed for others.

Jesus' death gives life to the world. The martyr's death gives life to all those who can feel and appreciate its testimony. The first martyrs modeled their witness on the life and death of Jesus, and in doing so they themselves became models of Christian holiness and heroism. They gave their all, and from their time to ours sainthood has been judged by the standard they set.

Confessors and Ascetics

The early centuries of systematic persecution came to an end in A.D. 313 when the Emperor Constantine issued an edict that Christianity was no longer illegal in the Roman Empire. Some later emperors tried to reverse the situation, and occasionally pagans were openly hostile to the new religion, but for the most part it was safe to be a Christian. Persecutions were not as frequent as they had been, and when they occurred they were not as severe. Martyrs were no longer as plentiful as they used to be, and Christians began to idealize another group of saints who were known as *confessors.*

When Catholics hear that word today, they usually assume that it has something to do with confession and the Sacrament of Reconciliation. Confessors in the early Church, however, were people who confessed that they were Christians, took the risk of being martyred but were not put to death. They practiced what we would call *civil disobedience*, refusing to renounce their allegiance to Christ even before threatening judges and angry crowds. They would not burn incense before pagan images; they would not fight in the army; they would not betray the names of other Christians. Sometimes they were imprisoned, beaten and tortured. But they were not killed, despite their confession of faith and heroic virtue.

As time went on, the term *confessor* was also applied to Christians who lived their faith heroically even when there was no threat of persecution. The very way they lived was seen as a confession of faith. In fact within a hundred years of Constantine's edict Christians were becoming the majority in the Roman Empire. Since it was now acceptable to be Christian, many people joined the Church who would never have done so when the cost of discipleship was higher. It was the beginning of what we have been calling cultural Christianity and ethnic Catholicism.

The later confessors were the countercultural Christians of their day. Just as the earlier confessors had risked martyrdom for their allegiance to Christ, these later confessors risked misunderstanding and even ridicule for the way they lived the gospel. If Christians were becoming soft, they believed that the Christian life should be tough. If Christians were becoming wealthy, they insisted that Jesus had called his followers to a poor and simple life. If Christians were getting caught up in the ways of the world, they thought that it was better to get out of society and live the gospel somewhere else. Perhaps they sometimes overstated their case, but they felt strongly that the case for discipleship had to be made. Because they did, they came to be regarded as saints.

Likely as not, these confessors would pack up their few belongings and hike out past the outskirts of the city to live alone. They became hermits or, as they are sometimes called, anchorites, because they renounced the world and stuck to their principles. They led an ascetical life, eating and sleeping very little, praying and fasting most of the time. That they could live without the comforts of society and enjoy living alone with the Lord was their witness to the truth that God is the source of all fulfillment and happiness.

The earliest of these confessors was actually born during the period of persecution but lived until well after it was over. He saw firsthand the change that took place in the Church when it became socially acceptable, and he yearned for the way that the gospel had been taken seriously in his youth. His name was Anthony the Abbot, and he decided to dedicate his life to God in the Egyptian desert. St. Anthony's reputation for holiness began to spread, however, and eventually a small group of disciples went to live near him to learn the way of total Christian commitment. He must have lived a healthy life, for when he died in 356 he was over 100 years old.

Not long afterward, another young man named Benedict took Anthony's idea a step further. Seeing the need for group support in living the Christian life, he composed a little book of rules for healthy community life. The Rule of St. Benedict has been the foundation of many monastic rules now for about 1,500 years. Prescribing a daily diet of prayer and work, St. Benedict's Rule struck a wholesome balance between strict asceticism and necessary human comforts. Within Benedict's own lifetime dozens of monasteries were founded for both men and women, and by the Middle Ages they numbered in the thousands. In earlier chapters we have seen how much communities of monks and nuns contributed to the Church through the centuries.

The monks and nuns typified those Christians who are willing to ask the ultimate gospel questions and live the answers in total confidence. They were Christian radicals in the sense that they went to the root of the gospel to find out what kind of life could grow from it. It would not be unfair to call them the first Christian dropouts from society, for they dropped out of mainstream Christianity to build community on an entirely different model from the ones they saw in the world. Monasteries were essentially Christian communes where people could practice radical discipleship in living the gospel. We sometimes forget that for about the first five centuries of their existence they were composed almost entirely of laymen and laywomen.

In our own day the Trappist monks exemplify this early ideal of monasticism. Most other orders in the Benedictine tradition live according to a more relaxed rule, but the Trappists still follow theirs rather strictly, including the rule of silence. They insist that to keep from getting caught up in the games that the world loves to play, one must live by very different rules and apart from the world.

This does not mean that the Trappists are unaware of what is going on in the world, or that they are uninvolved in it. Thomas Merton was a Trappist who influenced millions of people through his writings. Many of these were on prayer and spirituality, but towards the end of his life he was well ahead of most Catholics in his thinking on social justice. Ideas that he put forth in the 1960's about the arms race and nuclear weapons were picked up by the American hierarchy 20 years later.

We tend to think of the ascetical life as a withdrawal from the world. True, it is that, but that is only half of it. The withdrawal gives you the space to live the gospel freely, and from that freedom to speak to the world about what living the gospel really means. In that space you can discover the radical questions that Jesus poses to all who call themselves his followers, so that you can live the answers in true discipleship.

Many, if not most, saints have been ascetics in the sense that they practiced spiritual withdrawal or distancing from the world in order to look at it more objectively. Every now and then, though, we come across a holy person who led an obviously simple and withdrawn life. Such a person was Charles de Foucauld, a young man who turned his back on the sophistication of 19th-century France to live in a little hut in the Sahara Desert. He desired to live simply in a world that was becoming more and more complex and to understand the mystery of Jesus in a world that did not seem to comprehend it. His friends thought he was crazy, but he prayed above all else to experience the aloneness of Jesus in order to be in total communion with the Christ whom the world had rejected. He was willing to ask the ultimate gospel questions, and he wanted to do it where he was sure no one would be watching him. He did not want to put on a show for anyone, or be praised by anyone. He prayed only to find the answers and live them to the fullest.

Charles once wrote in his diary that he hoped to meet a violent end, just as Jesus did, and to die unrecognized and unappreciated. A few months later his body was found bloody and alone, apparently the victim of violent intruders on his solitude. Regardless of what we might think of his strange request, God seemed to answer his prayer.

He never knew that his spiritual legacy would be a community of Christians who came to admire the authenticity of his life and his devotion to the simplicity of the gospel. The Little Brothers of Jesus and the Little Sisters of Jesus, as they are known, live in tiny groups of two or three people in the poorest parts of the world. They are not widely known because they do not try to do anything great by the world's standards. Yet they are found all over Europe and Africa, Asia and America, and their numbers are growing. People are attracted to the simplicity of their life-style and the authenticity of their prayer life. They just try to live the gospel in the spirit of Charles de Foucauld, showing kindness and hospitality to people in need. They do not try to make converts, but there are always some who recognize the gospel truth of how they live and ask to join them.

Certainly theirs is a rare spiritual gift, a special charism. Not everyone is called by God to live the gospel that radically, but those who do live the gospel so authentically are a sign to us that it is both possible and wonderful. Their lives have a grace and beauty that eludes most of us. Their willingness to ask the ultimate questions forces us to ask whether we are really willing to face them.

The ascetics in the Church understand that the gospel is primarily a life-style. The institutional Church from the fourth century onward has tended to make the gospel a thought-style, a matter of doctrines and beliefs. The early anchorites and monks, however, were not concerned with doctrine but with living. Their argument was not with those who doubted the incarnation but with those who did not live a Jesus way of life. Their worry was not whether the Holy Spirit was a distinct Person in the Trinity but whether the Spirit was a vital force in Christian life. Theirs was not an intellectual search for doctrinal truth but a spiritual search for living truth.

The medieval paintings of St. Anthony in the desert often portray him surrounded by devils trying to tempt him. In our own day we are likely to think of these temptations in doctrinal and moral terms—not believing in God, disobeying the Commandments and the like. The real demons in most of our lives, however, are much more subtle than that. We believe in God, but we neglect to listen to the Lord in daily prayer. We obey the Commandments, but our minds are legalistic and cynical. We put some money in the collection every week, but we do not give ourselves to those who need us. We go to confession, but in our hearts we nurse jealousy and greed, bitterness and anger.

The ascetics remind us that we only come to know the Lord and know ourselves in solitude. When we have no social roles to play, we have to be ourselves. When all our public masks are stripped away, we begin to see the naked truth. When all our other support systems are removed, we discover whether we really trust in God. Do we confess our faith merely with our lips, or also with our lives? The saints we honor as heroes and heroines show us what it takes to ask the ultimate questions and to risk finding the fundamental answers about our life-style.

Founders

Many saints honored in the Church are founders of communities. Apart from those who have the charism to be anchorites or hermits, people who excel in holiness realize that faith-sharing, life-sharing and mission are essential to living the gospel. When they cannot find a group to support this vision, they often gather one around themselves.

In almost every century there were saints who either began communities or reformed existing ones. Often they started in solitude, listening to the Lord in prayer, until they realized that what God wanted them to do could not be done alone. They needed a support group and a task group to work at it, a Body of Christ whose members together could live Jesus in the world.

St. Augustine, the famous North African bishop who lived around the turn of the fifth century, saw the need for community among the deacons and priests of his diocese, and he invited some to live in a community near his cathedral. Although he did not start a religious order as such, the Augustinians were later founded in his spirit.

St. Dominic in the 13th century began with the vision of a mission: preaching the gospel to people in rural areas that had been neglected by the hierarchy. He scoured the cities for priests who were willing to join him. They lived on handouts and supported one another while they attended universities to get better training in theology. Although they are known popularly as Dominicans, their official name is the Order of Preachers.

St. Vincent de Paul and St. Louise de Marillac broke through traditional restrictions imposed on women until the 17th century. Women religious had always been expected to live in cloisters, protected by monastic walls, but Louise saw that there was a mission to be performed in the streets among the poor. With Vincent's support she broke with tradition, fought the hierarchy who opposed her novel idea and founded the Daughters of Charity. Vincent himself founded the Congregation of the Mission to work among the poor, and many parishes today have St. Vincent de Paul Societies in which laypeople carry on his mission in their neighborhoods.

St. Ignatius Loyola, a soldier recuperating from a battle wound, heard the Lord calling him to the service of the Church when Europe was being torn apart by the Reformation. He realized that if he was going to train an army of apostles to reform the Church and conquer the world for Christ, he would have to create a very different style of community. Until Ignatius's day, religious orders were organized along the lines of monasteries in which large groups lived together and prayed the Divine Office in the chapel every day. Ignatius sent his missionaries in groups of twos and threes and ordered them to pray a short form of the Office (the origin of today's Breviary) in private. He was criticized for this departure from tradition, but within a short while his Society of Jesus (or Jesuits, as they were called for short) was sending men to Africa and Asia and the Americas, performing missionary work on a scale unmatched in the history of the Church.

Founders of communities always have some insight into what the Church needs at a certain time, and they have a gift for meeting that need. Often the institutional Church does not perceive the need or does not agree on how to meet it, and the hierarchy tries to stifle the creative charism of the order. Some give up in the face of opposition, and their work does not last. But the communities willing to dialogue with the hierarchy and live in creative tension with the institution are able to pass on their gift to later generations.

The same sort of phenomenon is going on in the Church today. Laypeople are gathering into their own small communities, and often as not priests and bishops look upon them with suspicion. Yet, as we have seen in the previous chapter, the renewal of the Church is happening through the formation of communities, just as it always has in the history of the Church.

A quarter-century ago the Second Vatican Council told religious orders to reform themselves by returning to the charism of their founder, yet when the orders actually have done this the hierarchy have sometimes resisted. They bemoan the fact that nuns do not wear habits, forgetting that very often the habits were just the streetclothes of the times when the orders were founded. They decry the fact that priests and brothers are leaving large institutions empty, forgetting that very often the founders envisioned living in small communities. They demand that superiors be ordained priests in orders like the Franciscans when Francis himself refused ordination and would therefore not be able to be a superior in his own order today.

Founders are visionaries in the sense that they see new ways for communities to live the gospel when the old ways have gotten stale with routine. Founders are also radicals in the sense that they ask the most fundamental gospel questions of themselves and their followers. Institutions are often uncomfortable with visionaries and radicals, yet they can only be renewed by those who see what no one else yet sees. Fortunately for the Church, the hierarchy too has learned to live in creative tension with the founders of communities and those who believe in their radical vision of living the gospel.

Mystics

Mysticism in the Catholic tradition is the knowledge of God through experience. It is not head knowledge but heart knowledge, not intellectual comprehension but intuitive comprehension, not logical understanding but emotional understanding. It is the kind of awareness that develops between close friends, when one can tell almost instinctively what the other is thinking or feeling. Through their long hours of prayer, experiencing the presence of God, mystics develop that same kind of sensitive awareness to what the Lord wants of them.

When mystics write about their experience of God, they speak a very different language from the language of theology and doctrine. They speak what can best be called religious poetry, a language of symbolism and imagery and feeling. Ordinary words cannot describe what they are experiencing, so mystics stretch the meaning of words beyond their ordinary usage. Needless to say, when they do this they often are misunderstood by those who do not have such experiences themselves. They have even sometimes been condemned as heretics because they did not use theological language "correctly."

For this reason, although some mystics have been canonized as saints, many more have not. This lack of official recognition by the institutional Church, however, has not prevented Christians from recognizing mystics as heroes and heroines of contemplative prayer.

Meister Eckhart, who lived in the 14th century, was one of those mystics who got in trouble for making poetically paradoxical statements about God. Talking about his prayer life, for example, he said, "I pray God to rid me of God." On the surface, this sounds like Eckhart is asking God to make him an atheist! But this is not what he means at all. What he is trying to say in one short sentence is that to go deeper in our experience of God we have to ask God to rid ourselves of false images of God. Eckhart wants to experience God nakedly and honestly, and so he prays to be stripped of all the masks we put on God to avoid facing the utter otherness of infinite mystery.

On a different occasion, Eckhart said, "The eyes by which we look at God are the very same eyes by which he first looks at us." That sounds paradoxical, yet it is profoundly mystical. We come to understand its meaning only after we discover what it names in our own prayer experience. The reality is hard to put into words, but it means something like the desire we have for God is itself a gift from God, or the love we have for God is already God loving in us.

St. Teresa of Avila and St. John of the Cross were two Spanish mystics of the 16th century who were eventually canonized, but during their lifetimes they were often at odds with the Church leaders who mistrusted their renewal of the religious life. Typical mystics, they spoke and acted directly from their prayer life, and their actions were often perceived as threatening the institutional system. Because mystics experience great inner freedom from institutional structures, their humility and loyalty to the Church are often tested to the limit.

St. Thérèse of Lisieux, popularly known as the Little Flower of Jesus, never got in trouble for what she said and did, perhaps because she was so genuine and unpretentious. She did not challenge any religious authorities but went about her daily tasks in a continuous attitude of reverence for Christ. Her writings attracted a wide audience in the 20th century because they were disarmingly simple yet profoundly mystical.

Speaking about the guilt and negativity that people sometimes carry within them, she said, "Whoever is willing to serenely bear the trial of being displeasing to himself, that person will be a pleasant place of shelter for Jesus." Most of us try to suppress our guilt feelings and escape from feeling bad about ourselves, but through her relationship to Christ, Thérèse learned a more honest and healthy practice. Face up to our sins and failures, she said, and remember that God loves us despite them. If we admit our brokenness, we can allow Jesus to come in and heal us. She learned that through mystical prayer—a hundred years before psychotherapy discovered the healthiness of self-knowledge and self-acceptance.

Pierre Teilhard de Chardin was a Jesuit priest and scientist, a poet and mystic who lived in our own century. Since he wrote about evolution before most church people had accepted that idea, he got in trouble with the hierarchy. Most of his works were not published until after his death. When we read them we can see how his mystical intuition blended religion and science, poetry and reason. They are beautiful to read but difficult to comprehend. Mystics think and feel at depths that are unfamiliar to most of us.

The mystics' sense of time is timeless, as it is for God. Past, present and future are united in a flash of mystical insight. They speak of Jesus' crucifixion as though it were happening today, or they see events to come as though they were going on right now. The same is true of the mystics' sense of space. In their religious experience heaven and earth are one reality, and the distinction between the natural and the supernatural disappears. Everything comes together into unity, even as it does for God, who encompasses all time and space within a single divine embrace.

Caryll Houselander, an English mystic who also lived in this century, is a wonderful example of this. When she was a young woman she had several profoundly mystical experiences through which she saw the world for the rest of her life. One day while riding in a London subway, she looked around and saw Christ in every person that she looked at. From this she realized that Christ is in every person in every country in every century.

Another time, shortly after the Communists had taken over Russia, she looked at a newspaper photo of the assassinated czar and saw Christ again, his crown of thorns replacing the czar's crown of gold. Raising her eyes, she beheld a huge Russian icon of Christ spread over the city, and she felt a deep conviction that it would be through

Russia that Christ would return to redeem the world. Catholics have prayed for decades for the conversion of Russia, and perhaps those prayers will be answered in a way that we least expect. One mystic, at least, saw a symbolic vision of its coming true.

Mystics are a special gift to the Church because they show us how far we can go in prayer, or rather, how far God will take us if we allow ourselves to be led in prayer. They are the heroes and heroines of the prayer dimension of the Christian life, for they courageously open themselves to the fullest human experience of God. They reveal to us the deepest meaning of conversion, which is the total transformation of our life through union with Christ.

Thinkers

Sometimes saints do not fall easily into the categories we have created for understanding where they stand in the spectrum of holiness. St. Thomas Aquinas, for example, was a theologian all his life, but a month before he died he had a mystical experience that made all his years of thinking seem insignificant to him. "It's as worthless as a pile of straw," he is reported to have said. Perhaps so, but Thomas's straw provided fuel for Catholic theology for centuries after him.

In the calendar of saints the thinkers and intellectuals are usually referred to as doctors of the Church. They were Ph.D.'s in theology, so to speak, even before universities started granting degrees. The word *doctor* in Latin simply means one who teaches, and the Church has learned a lot from these teachers.

About half of the canonized doctors of the Church lived during the first centuries, and they were instrumental in formulating the basic doctrines of the faith, such as those found in the Creed. Many others lived in the Middle Ages, at the time when the oldest universities of Europe were being founded. Since the main subjects taught in these new schools were philosophy and theology, they set the standards for western intellectual life which have been the hallmarks of scholarship ever since. They grappled with the great issues of their day: moral and political, individual and social, scientific and religious. The university was the place where all knowledge came together to be examined, discussed and passed on to the next generation of scholars.

St. Anselm, who lived in the 11th century, was one of the first of these medieval scholars. He is the one who defined *theology* as "faith seeking understanding," balancing the claims of those who said all we need is faith against the claims of those who said that science is everything. Ever since Anselm, Catholicism has had a healthy respect for the role of reason in religion. Blind faith is not the way to live the Christian life, he said, for if it were God would not have given us minds to think with.

St. Thomas Aquinas and St. Bonaventure both lived in the 13th century, at the height of medieval university life. Both wrote great works attempting to put together what was known through divine revelation and what was known through human investigation. Bonaventure was also an administrator in the Franciscan Order, so he did not write as much as Thomas, but both carried on the agenda that Anselm had set for Catholic theology.

Although Thomas's *Summa Theologica* later became a standard textbook in Catholic seminaries, during his lifetime his work was anything but uncontroversial. While he was just a student in Paris, the works of the Greek philosopher Aristotle were being rediscovered. Thomas found much that was truthful in them, but the conservatives of the day attacked him for trying to use the ideas of an atheist in doing Christian theology.

That same battle, in one form or another, has been waged over and over again in the history of theology. One by one, however, the new insights of astronomy, archaeology, evolution, ethics, politics, psychology and many other disciplines have been integrated into Christian thought through the efforts of courageous intellectuals. They were convinced that since there is one Author of the universe, there can ultimately be no contradiction between religion and science. Time has proven that they were correct, and we are the beneficiaries of their steadfast conviction. Catholicism has been immensely enriched by the faith and scholarship of such thinkers.

In our own day that battle is being fought on a number of fronts, most notably on the one that usually makes the headlines—liberation theology. Thinkers such as Gustavo Gutierrez and Leonardo Boff have been criticized for using some of the ideas of Karl Marx in their writings. Since Marx was an atheist and his critique of Western society was adopted by Communism, some feel that his ideas can have no place in theology.

Catholic intellectuals do not always have to fight to have their ideas accepted, however. Sometimes the sheer scope and scholarship of their thought is enough to win them respect. Karl Rahner and Bernard Lonergan are two such thinkers whose work showed the Catholic world that theology could successfully integrate modern philosophy and science into a broad intellectual synthesis. To some extent, we owe the success of the Second Vatican Council to thinkers such as these who helped the bishops see that the Church could move into more modern ways of expressing its faith.

Unfortunately, since women in the past were excluded from university education, there are only two female doctors of the Church. St. Teresa of Avila was proclaimed the first woman doctor of the Church and St. Catherine of Siena the second in 1970. As women enter more fully into the intellectual life of Catholicism, they will undoubtedly make great contributions. We saw in Chapter Two that the spiritual temperament of Catholicism is fundamentally feminine, but this dimension of human life has yet to be fully integrated into theology.

Thinkers, intellectuals, writers, teachers—some have been officially recognized as saints and some have not. Many of them, though, have had heroic faith, and the Church has benefitted from their persistent search to understand the implications of that faith.

Activists

At the other end of the spectrum from academics are the activists, the people who go out and make things happen. Instead of writing about the Christian faith, they live it to the utmost. Many of the confessors and founders could be placed within this category, but some of the confessors were reclusive contemplatives, and not all activists have founded their own communities. We need another category, then, for those heroes and heroines who have found their fulfillment in the active living of the gospel.

Missionary saints come to mind first. St. Patrick in the fifth century and St. Columba in the sixth dedicated their lives to bringing Christianity and civilization to the Celtic tribes of Ireland and Scotland. Although they established many monasteries in the British Isles, they were not intending to found new religious orders but to set up centers of Christian living from which other missionaries could be sent.

Many of the missionaries who in turn converted western Europe were Celtic monks, descendants of the early converts. St. Columban spread the faith through France and Switzerland before he died in northern Italy in the seventh century. St. Boniface left a comfortable monastery in England to ask Pope Gregory II for permission to be a missionary. The pope consecrated Boniface a bishop and sent him into Germany, where he directed the great missionary effort of the eighth century.

Saints Cyril and Methodius were two brothers who undertook in eastern Europe what the Celtic monks had accomplished in the West. They left their home in Greece to preach the gospel in Bulgaria, Czechoslovakia, Poland and Russia. Like the monks before them, they brought not only Christianity but also civilization to their converts. They translated the Bible into Slavic, and invented an alphabet in order to so, for, until that time, Slavic had been an unwritten language.

After the conversion of Europe was completed, we do not read much more of missionaries until after the discovery that the earth was round—and inhabited by people who had not yet heard of Christ. In the 15th century the Church renewed its missionary efforts, sending mainly Franciscans and Jesuits into Asia and the Americas, although in time many other missionary orders were founded as well.

St. Francis Xavier exhausted himself converting thousands to Christianity in India and Japan, where he died before he had even reached 50 years old. Bartolomé de las Casas lived most of his life in Spain, but when he visited South America and saw how the Spanish were enslaving the Indians, he dedicated his life to writing and arguing in the courts that such brutality was contrary to the gospel.

St. Isaac Jogues returned to Christianize the Iroquois Indians in present-day New York, even after they had tortured him and mangled his hands during his first missionary journey. Needless to say, he died a martyr's death. Quite a different fate awaited Junipero Serra, who was sent out west to preach the gospel. He lived to a happy old age, but the amazing fact of his story is that he did not even begin his journey up and down the California coast until he was 55, an age when many people start looking forward to retirement. Many of the missions that he founded grew into the great cities of California: San Francisco, Santa Clara, San Diego and others.

Not all missionary work, of course, is done in foreign lands. We already have spoken of St. Vincent de Paul's mission to the poor in Europe, and we can balance that by mentioning some of those who undertook the same apostolate in the United States. St. Elizabeth Ann Seton saw the need of poor children in cities for Catholic education, and St. Katherine Drexel saw the same need of black and Indian children in the South and West. In the spirit of St. Louise de Marillac, both Elizabeth and Katherine encouraged other women to join them in their mission, and they founded two of the great teaching orders in our country, the Sisters of Charity and the Sisters of the Blessed Sacrament.

Dorothy Day would never have dreamed of starting a religious order, but she did begin the Catholic Worker movement with Peter Maurin in New York in the 1930's. She saw that the basic cause of poverty is the unjust economic system in which the poor are forced to live, and she dedicated her life not just to feeding the poor and sheltering the homeless but also to fighting for fair wages and better working conditions. She led a very active Christian life right up to the end of her 83 years.

Activists often are not popular with their contemporaries. Countless missionaries besides the ones of which we have spoken died as martyrs. Bartolomé de las Casas made enemies in the courts of Spain for defending the human rights of the Indians, as did other less famous Franciscans and Jesuits who also pleaded the cause of the oppressed. During her lifetime Dorothy Day often was reviled as a socialist and communist because she criticized the systemic evils of capitalism.

In our own day the most visible activists are those who protest the arms race in our own country and those who fight for political and economic justice in South Africa and Latin America.

Many of them are dedicated laypeople; many too are nuns and priests. When they insist that the gospel is not good news to the poor unless it also frees them from oppression, they are labeled as subversives and traitors. As Dom Helder Camara, an archbishop in Brazil, observed, "As long as I feed the poor, they call me a saint; but if I ask *why* they are poor, they call me a communist."

We forget that when Jesus preached the gospel to the poor, he too made enemies. He was labeled as a blasphemer by the religious establishment, but in the end he was put to death by the political establishment. Could it be that the Romans and their Jewish counterparts saw the revolutionary implications of the gospel which we tend to overlook? Could this be why in every age the poor and weak have accepted the gospel more readily than the rich and powerful? The social activists in the Church, both past and present, believe the answer to those questions is yes.

An Old Testament image of the messiah that was applied to Jesus in the New Testament was that of the Suffering Servant. Activist heroes and heroines believe that to be like

Jesus Christians ought to dedicate their lives to helping others, even to the point of suffering. Like Jesus, they lay down their lives and, if necessary, give them up for the world's salvation.

Humanists

From the stories we have told so far, it might appear that it is impossible to be a saint without doing something extraordinarily different from what most people do. To a great extent this is true, but it is not the whole truth. Some people become heroes to others by doing ordinary things with extraordinary faith in God. For lack of a better name, we might call them Christian humanists. They lead active lives, but they are not missionaries or social activists. They lead dedicated lives, but they are not necessarily dedicated to an unusual cause.

Perhaps the best example of such a saint is Thomas More. A lawyer by profession with a wife and family, his many talents brought him to prominence in 16th-century England. Besides being a practical businessman, he was also a philosopher and writer, he loved music and he patronized the arts. King Henry VIII admired Thomas More's honesty and administrative skill and appointed him Chancellor of the Realm. When Henry decided that to divorce his wife he would have to make himself the head of the Church of England, almost all the nobles and bishops agreed that the move was politically necessary. Thomas, however, refused to go along, his loyalty to the pope was branded as treason, and he was executed for obeying his conscience.

The saints we are calling humanists are whole and integrated people. They are able to balance mind and heart, science and art, religion and politics in a fully human life. As a matter of historical fact, however, such education and personal development was available only to the relatively wealthy. For this reason, some of these saints are members of the aristocracy.

St. Elizabeth of Hungary was married to a nobleman

whom she loved very deeply, and she used her position and influence to distribute food and clothing to the impoverished peasants in her husband's lands. After her husband was killed in a war, she saw to it that her children were taken care of and then joined the Third Order of St. Francis to spend the rest of her days in poverty and prayer. She lived a full life, even though she was only 24 when she died.

St. Louis IX of France, like Elizabeth, lived in the 13th century at the height of the Middle Ages. He too was married, and he lived long enough to have 10 children. He vowed to be a good Christian king, and he was loved by his people for his honesty in government and his generosity to the poor. His sense of duty to God inspired him to lead a crusade to free the Holy Land from Muslim control. His long and varied career shows how possible it is to be saintly despite the temptations of power and prestige.

St. Francis de Sales was a bishop in French-speaking Switzerland at the time of the Reformation. Forced out of Geneva by the Protestants, he spent much of his time as a spiritual director to laypeople, especially women. He counseled them on how to develop their relationship with God even though they led active lives as wives and mothers with social responsibilities. Going against the tradition that only those who left the world could truly follow Christ, he wrote letters and books encouraging people to remain in the world and lead devout Christian lives.

Although St. Philip Neri came from a well-to-do family in Italy, he decided to make his own living in 16th-century Rome. An active layman, he gathered a community of young men around him who worked among the poor and sick. Only when he was 35 was he persuaded that it might be better to be ordained a priest and to have his community recognized as a religious order. The Oratorians, however, were different from the other orders of the time in that they lived in community without taking the traditional monastic vows, so that they might work better in the world while trying to make it a better place.

When John Henry Newman became a convert to Catholicism in 19th-century England, he was an Anglican priest with a reputation for being a fine preacher and careful scholar. His research into early Church history, however, led him to the conclusion that if he wanted to belong to the Church of the apostles he would have to join the Church that was headed by the pope. Desiring to be a Catholic priest, he decided that the Oratory founded by St. Philip Neri well suited his academic life-style. For many years he studied and wrote in relative seclusion, until Pope Leo XIII made him a cardinal and brought his work to the attention of the whole Catholic world.

Many of the saints that we would have to classify as humanists were administrators in the Church or, as they are more commonly referred to, bishops. Even though they were priests, their day-to-day lives were busy with the practical running of their dioceses, just as the lives of bishops are today. Very often, the bishops who have been canonized as saints were great reformers in the Church, and their ability as administrators led to their being elected pope.

St. Ambrose was bishop of Milan in Italy towards the end of the fourth century, when the barbarians were beginning to invade the Roman Empire. So many government services were disrupted that bishops stepped in and began to provide orphanages, hospitals and old-age homes to relieve the social distress. Ambrose went even further than most bishops in identifying with his people, eating daily with the poor and refusing to use gold altar vessels in the cathedral as long as there were captives who could be ransomed by selling the gold. Ambrose also stood up for human rights when they were violated by the Roman government under the pretext of national security.

Another bishop famous for his humanitarian aid to those in need and for his defense of the Church against the power of the state was St. Thomas Becket in 12th-century England. Although he had been the king's handpicked candidate for archbishop of Canterbury, Thomas Becket put his allegiance to Christ ahead of his loyalty to the crown, and in the end he was martyred in his own cathedral by government agents, just as Oscar Romero was in El Salvador not long ago.

Two of the great humanist popes were both named

Gregory. Gregory I was an educated layman who had renounced his wealth and political ambitions, only to be chosen by the people to be bishop of Rome. He led the Church through the turmoil at the end of the sixth century, bringing peace to central Italy, sending missionaries to convert the barbarians in Europe and sponsoring a reform of the liturgy. The type of church music he favored became known as Gregorian chant, and it was so well suited to the liturgy that it was widely used until the 20th century.

Gregory VII was a monk who was elected pope in the 11th century, at a time when many monasteries and dioceses were in dire need of reform. As a monk he endorsed the renewal of monasteries by returning to the spirit of St. Benedict. As pope he made sure that priests performed their pastoral duties, that bishops did not become pawns of kings and that the Church was well administered. Through his vision and leadership, the papacy became a major force of civilization in the Middle Ages.

Unfortunately for the history of the Church, great humanist popes were not always very saintly. The popes just prior to the Protestant Reformation were more interested in increasing the magnificence of the Vatican than in governing the Church wisely. The result was a widespread protest that has left the Church divided ever since. It is not easy to be "in the world yet not of the world," as Jesus counseled his disciples to be. It is all too easy to fall into the ways of the world, even if one is working for the Church.

In our own day the Church has been fortunate to have popes who have impressed even non-Catholics with their humanness. Pope John XXIII stepped down from the pedestal that popes had been placed on for centuries and showed how down-to-earth a saint can be. He walked around the city of Rome, visited prisoners in jails and joked with reporters. When asked why he had summoned the Second Vatican Council, he walked over to a large window, dramatically threw it open, and explained, "To let in a little fresh air!" He addressed his last encyclical, *Pacem in Terris*, not just to Catholics but to people of goodwill everywhere who desire peace on earth.

Pope John Paul II is a humanist by his own admission, having been a poet and playwright and a personalist philosopher. He speaks a half-dozen languages fluently, and he has traveled around the globe to make the papacy more real for Catholics everywhere. He writes constantly about the needs of people in the modern world, appealing not only to Church teachings but also to the common humanity of all God's children as the basis of our concern. He speaks frequently and bravely about the rights of the poor to be freed from political and economic oppression.

Even though not all the great Christian humanists have been canonized as saints, they are heroes and heroines of the Church because they exemplify a style of sanctity to which well-to-do and educated people can aspire. They put together in a holistic way the best that the world has to offer with the gifts that God has given them, showing the many benefits of fully integrating the human and the divine.

Eccentrics

As if to reassure us that it is possible to be a saint without being totally balanced, as the humanists are, the Church has always recognized a number of Christians for their holiness despite their nuttiness. People at the time might have thought them crazy, but in retrospect (often only after their death) they saw that these saints were madly in love with God. Because their hearts were totally surrendered to the Lord, these eccentric individuals did not care about what other people thought of them. They lived only for God, in the way that God revealed was right for them, even if no one else wanted to live that way.

We do not usually think of St. John the Baptist as an eccentric, but he undoubtedly was. The New Testament tells us that he lived in the desert dressed in animal skins, and that he ate insects and wild honey to keep alive. He told people straight off that they were sinners and they ought to repent, and for good measure he dunked them in the Jordan River if they believed him. When the religious leaders of his day came by to see what he was doing, he called them a bunch of snakes and hypocrites. Were he alive today, John would not be the kind of saint who would be welcome in most parishes.

St. Benedict Joseph Labré was a bit gentler in his appearance than John was, but he was just as dirty and he smelled just as bad. He was a sort of Christian hobo in 18th-century France, sleeping in open fields or under bridges when it rained. When most people saw him coming they crossed over to the other side of the road, afraid that he would ask them for a handout. Those who let him get close to them, however, saw great serenity in his eyes and felt great healing power in his hands.

St. Joseph Cupertino was a Franciscan friar whose claim to fame was the odd habit of levitating while he prayed. If you visit the monastery in Italy where he lived in the 17th century, the guide will even show you some patches in the ceiling where Joseph is supposed to have knocked off the plaster while in the heights of prayer! Apparently he always landed safely, though, and so he was named the patron saint of aviators.

St. Simeon Stylites wanted to abandon the world and live closer to God, so he perched on a marble column and stayed there day and night. His was not the healthiest of life-styles, to be sure, and perhaps he was even a bit of a fanatic. Yet this lone figure atop a pillar became a symbol in the fifth century of total dedication to God, and people used to come from miles around to request that he pray for them when they sent up the offerings that he lived on.

Brother Juniper, one of the first Franciscans, had a childlike spirit and, even though he has never been officially canonized, he was recognized for his holiness during his own lifetime. He did frivolous things like play with children on seesaws and run merrily through the middle of town, not at all the way a mature friar is supposed to behave. He is remembered for having been a close friend of St. Francis, yet today we have to wonder whether someone who behaved like that would be considered too eccentric to belong to a religious order.

Because the eccentrics are so out of the ordinary, they

throw into high relief what it means to be a saint. Unlike the humanists, you cannot confuse their holiness with personal accomplishment. Personally they did not accomplish anything great, but they allowed something great to be accomplished in them. They allowed the Spirit to take over their lives, and their lives showed that spiritual greatness is not measured by merely human standards. Like the ascetics who were mentioned earlier, the eccentrics followed the Lord wherever he led them, and he led them all the way to happiness.

Exemplars

Some saints stand out before all the world. Even people who are not Catholics, or who are not Christians perhaps, see in their lives a spiritual greatness that is as deep as it is broad. They see dedication and conviction, purity and loyalty, love and openness that are rare by human standards. They personify a fire that illuminates not just Catholic history but all of human history with the example of what one person can do to touch the lives of others and transform them for the good.

In our own day, Pope John XXIII and Thomas Merton have been such heroes. John, with his honesty and humor, enabled Catholics to take a good hard look at their own Church, laugh at its medieval foibles and work for its renewal. By his willingness to reach out to people of other faiths, he inspired a renewed search for religious unity and mutual understanding that is still going on today. Merton had a much more uncompromising personality, but his singleness of purpose spoke to people who knew little about monastic life, and his wholehearted opposition to war attracted many to the cause of peace.

Saints such as Peter and Paul are recognized even by Christian denominations which do not recognize the process of canonization. Peter the fisherman and Paul the tentmaker exemplify what it means to have your whole life touched and turned around by Christ.

Peter promised more than he could deliver; he bragged about his loyalty to Jesus but he did not understand what was being asked of him. In a moment of crisis he collapsed under pressure. But he did not give up. He turned again to Jesus, asked for forgiveness and received from God the strength he did not have within himself to preach conversion and forgiveness to others.

Paul was so zealous for God's law that he even persecuted the followers of Jesus whom he thought had abandoned it. Yet he was open to an entirely different understanding of what God wanted of him, and in a blinding vision he saw that he was persecuting the very Lord whom he had vowed to obey. In that moment he became obedient to a higher law, and he dedicated the rest of his life to bringing others into the community of love that Jesus revealed to him.

Mary, the mother of Jesus, is such an exemplar of holiness that often we do not even think of her as a saint. We give her titles such as the Blessed Virgin or the Mother of God, forgetting that in England she is called St. Mary and that in the Latin countries she is called Santa Maria. In his Gospel St. Luke depicts Mary as the first among the disciples, the one who understood from the beginning what it means to give up everything in answer to God's call. "May it be done to me according to your word" (Luke 1:38), Mary's answer to the annunciation that she was to be the mother of the messiah, typifies the total response that everyone is called to make to God. Her presence with Jesus at the cross exemplifies the willingness we all must have to suffer patiently, trusting beyond human hope in the promise of God's Kingdom.

Although this brief list of exemplary saints is no more exhaustive than the ones that preceded it, it could not be complete without mentioning St. Francis of Assisi. More has been written about St. Francis than about any other saint in human history. Perhaps this is because he falls into so many of the categories that we have been describing that it is impossible to classify him except by calling him an exemplar of Christian holiness.

From the moment of his conversion as a rich young man to be a follower of Christ, Francis lived the life of an ascetic.

He died at age 44, his body showing the strain that years of self-denial had engraved on it. He was undeniably eccentric, from the day that he took off all his clothes in the public square to renounce the trappings of the world, to the months he spent in rebuilding an abandoned chapel in Assisi, to the times that he was overheard preaching to the birds and animals. Yet the very nonsense of the way that he had chosen to live attracted others to his way of life, and despite himself he became the founder of not one but three religious orders that bear his name.

There was no happier man in all of medieval Christendom, yet all he claimed to be doing was living the gospel. This simple confession of faith, lived wholeheartedly, ranks him with the great confessors of the Church. He risked martyrdom by walking unarmed into Muslim territory during the Crusades, but the Saladin recognized the holiness of this crazy Christian. Nevertheless, he meditated continuously on the sufferings of Christ during his long hours of mystical prayer, and he united himself so intimately with his wounded Lord that towards the end of his life his body was bruised with the marks of Jesus' crucifixion.

Francis would never have claimed to be a thinker, yet his thought, simple and straightforward as it was, has touched more lives than the writings of the educated doctors of the Church. And his humanness, uncomplicated and direct as it was, has spoken more eloquently to millions than the monumental works of the great humanists in Christianity.

Francis in the Middle Ages, Mary and the great apostles at the beginning, and whomever we might care to nominate as modern exemplars of sanctity, are the kinds of models that we all need to be inspired to holiness. They are the living proof of the living truth of the good news that we call the gospel. They show us what we all can be, and what we are all called to be, as followers of Jesus.

Catholicism and the Challenge of Sanctity

Whenever and wherever they lived, the saints were always free. They were free to love, for by loving God wholeheartedly their love embraced all of God's creation, and by allowing God's love to take possession of their hearts their love extended to everyone that God loves. They were free to live, for by living only for God they were liberated from lesser concerns, and by allowing God to live in them they became all that God wanted them to be. They were free to be poor, for by opening themselves to God they knew that nothing else could satisfy them, and by accepting God as their greatest treasure they had all the riches they could ever want.

All the same, such freedom has a price. Such grace does not come cheaply. If it did, we would all be saints and the saints would not be the heroes and heroines that they are. The saints found the pearl of great price that is mentioned in the Gospels, and they were willing to sell all they had to possess it. In our little sketches we had to leave out many details in the saints' lives. When we read about those lives in detail, however, we see that the saints became free, loving, happy and fulfilled people only through years of struggle.

Their lives are a challenge for each of us to join that struggle. It is, first of all, a struggle within. Each of us has a self that wants to be self-centered, that wants to have its desires satisfied, that wants to be in control of its own destiny. The struggle with such temptations is symbolized by the demons that torment St. Anthony in the desert. Something within us does not want to give up being selfish, yet it is only by becoming selfless that we are freed from the demands of the self. Something about us does not want to surrender self-direction, yet it is only by surrendering to God that we are directed toward our greatest happiness—the freedom to love wholeheartedly and without reservation.

The struggle, secondly, is with the world around us. The world is filled with good things, but so often the good is the enemy of the best. The saints often faced family and friends who told them to be satisfied with just being good, just

144

obeying the Commandments, just going to church and leading a decent life, just making a living and getting along like everybody else. They had to struggle with that temptation just to be good instead of reaching out for holiness. The saints also had to struggle with political and social forces that tried to make them conform to what is socially acceptable. In the face of that opposition they risked being outcasts for their faith, and sometimes they were martyred for it. Ironically, many saints also struggled with the institutional Church, whose representatives did not always appreciate their authentic holiness. To their credit, the saints surrendered to God's demands rather than to ecclesiastical pressures, and to the Church's credit, it ultimately recognized the gospel authenticity of their lives.

To return to the point from which we started in Chapter One, the great tradition of Catholicism is ultimately a tradition of saintliness. It is a tradition of a people and a church, to be sure, but that tradition is like a sea of holiness whose tide rises on waves of spiritual renewal. On the caps of those waves stand the saints, who have been drawn further upward than most and who pull the rest toward greater self-transcendence. The saints stand on the tradition that supports them, leading the way upward toward the infinite emptiness that the mystics say is filled with God.

Catholicism at its best wants people not just to admire saints but to be saints. It is a tradition that holds forth its saints as heroes and heroines because Catholicism is not something to know but a way to live. It is a way to live fully and freely and lovingly, as the saints did.

To enter that tradition is to embark upon a journey, a search for wisdom to live the way God wants each of us to live. To participate in that tradition is to follow in the footsteps of Abraham and Sarah, Moses and Miriam, Judith and the prophets of the Old Testament, Mary and the disciples of the New Testament and the centuries of saints who have propelled the Judeo-Christian tradition forward with their lives. To embrace that tradition is to make that journey ours and to turn their quest for holiness into our own.

The reason to be Catholic, ultimately, is to be a saint. The saints who have gone before us point the way. They show that it can be done and how it can be done. Their lives are not meant to be slavishly copied, but they are given to us as inspirations for the future. They give us patterns according to which we can design our own lives on our way to becoming saints. Yet just as each of the saints was different from the others, so each of us can expect to be different from all the rest.

The Church has nothing to gain from living in the past. If the saints become just the names of parishes and the names we give our children, the Catholic tradition will become a thing of the past. Some of the greatest saints had names that no saint had before them. Some of the holiest Catholics did and said and wrote things that no Jew or Christian had before them. The saints who are alive today carry on that great tradition of creative holiness.

If the wisdom of Catholicism is depicted in its saints, then the challenge of Catholicism is that each and every one of us should be like them in our own way. We must individually and together imagine how to live the gospel authentically, and then we must commit ourselves to putting that vision into practice.

The gospel was good news for the saints and the world in which they lived. If the gospel is to be good news for us and our world as well, we must live it as radically as did the saints.

Other books by Richard Rohr and Joseph Martos...

The Great Themes of Scripture: Old Testament

In six chapters—"The Call: Introduction to the Word," "Exodus: The Journey of Faith," "Joshua to Kings: The Ordinary Becomes the Extraordinary," "The Prophets: Radical Traditionalists," "Genesis and Job: God and Humankind, Good and Evil" and "Salvation History: Faith in Evolution"—the authors show the story of the Hebrew Scriptures as one of promise and fulfillment, hope and love. **SBN 853 $5.95**

The Great Themes of Scripture: New Testament

In seven chapters—"Matthew's Good News: The Reign of God," "Mark and John's Good News: Jesus Is Lord," "Luke and Acts: The Gift of the Spirit," "Mary, Prayer and the Church: Let It Be," "Paul: A New Creation," "Apocalypse: The New Jerusalem" and "Our New Jerusalem: A Modern Faith Journey"—the authors outline the story of Jesus and his message. **SBN 985 $6.95**

Available from St. Anthony Messenger Press, 1615 Republic St., Cincinnati, OH 45210. Call toll-free 1-800-336-1770.